心悦雅集

玉麟舍藏　傅熹年署檢

佳品荟萃，

堪酬挚友。

高山流水，

以谢知音。

心 悦 雅 集

Objects of Art from and for the Heart

主　编：黑静麟　马燕梅

Compiled by Hei Jinglin and Ma Yanmei

故宫出版社

The Forbidden City Publishing House

图书在版编目（ＣＩＰ）数据

心悦雅集 ：汉英对照 ／ 黑静麟，马燕梅主编． --
北京 ：故宫出版社，2012.5
　ISBN 978-7-5134-0261-3

Ⅰ．①心… Ⅱ．①黑… ②马… Ⅲ．①收藏 - 中国 - 图
集　Ⅳ．① G894-64

中国版本图书馆 CIP 数据核字（2012）第 077937 号

心悦雅集

主　　编 ：黑静麟　马燕梅
责任编辑 ：刘　辉　李园明
装帧设计 ：郑子杰
出版发行 ：故宫出版社
　　　　地址 ：北京东城区景山前街 4 号　邮编 ：100009
　　　　电话 ：010-85007808　010-85007816　传真 ：010-65129479
　　　　网址 ：www.culturefc.cn　邮箱 ：ggcb@culturefc.cn
印　　刷 ：北京雅昌彩色印刷有限公司
开　　本 ：285×285 毫米 1/12
印　　张 ：20.5
图　　版 ：360 幅
版　　次 ：2012 年 5 月第 1 版
　　　　　2012 年 5 月第 1 次印刷
印　　数 ：1 ~ 2000 册
书　　号 ：ISBN 978-7-5134-0261-3
定　　价 ：300.00 元

前言

王亚民

　　中国的收藏历史源远流长，最早可追溯到东晋，参与者大多是既有政治地位又有鉴赏水平和富余财力的士大夫阶层。王、谢、桓等名门望族，常把鉴藏艺术品的多寡作为衡量门户高低的尺度之一，当时士大夫如桓玄等，都是收藏巨富之人。其后刘宋、萧齐、萧梁均有继承发展，鉴藏之风延续未断。张彦远自其高祖辈起五代富于收藏，成为其编写《历代名画记》的坚实基础。米芾父子及王诜等众多兼具书画家身份的士大夫或贵戚参与收藏，也是前朝所未及。元代柯九思、倪瓒均以诗、书、画之"三绝"名重当时，同时也都精于鉴赏，家藏颇丰。

　　属清宫旧藏的精品很多是清乾隆内府《石渠宝笈》著录的藏品，表面看来这些国宝是乾隆皇帝以帝王势力毫不费力搜罗而来的，实际上却有很大一部分是梁清标、安岐等几个收藏家对明末散佚书画珍品鉴定收藏的成果积累。及至近代，如果没有张伯驹、孙瀛洲、陈万里等收藏大家的出现，中国的很多宝物恐怕摆脱不掉或流散海外或毁于动乱的命运。正是有他们对大量散佚文物的保护和其后向故宫博物院的文物捐赠，才使今天的我们有幸一睹这些艺术瑰宝的庐山真面目。

　　如今中国古代艺术品拍卖及收藏市场的异常火爆不再能以单纯的"盛世收藏"来注解，而是更多的体现出一个民族对自己文化的认同和尊重。收藏家对当今世界发展的理性思考，以对中国传统文化优越性的深切感受，整个收藏因此转向更具内涵的层面。此时出版此书籍来鼓励、宣传并引导收藏就极富意义。

　　正因如此，故宫博物院所属故宫出版社编辑出版此系列，希望此书能够为学者带来研究的实物资料，为欣赏者呈现不同时期的文化宝藏，此书将成为广大读者提供增强民族自豪感和爱国主义热情的良好教材。

目录

Contents

序一

张如兰

初识黑静麟、马燕梅夫妇，不觉半点特殊，谈吐举止，谦恭自牧。唯每每谈及玉之话题，夫妇二人，顿时神采奕然，话如泉涌，心悦之感，跃然眉宇。

这对藏美玉不计其数的恩爱伉俪，虽未出身名门望族，但与玉石之交，夫妇二人家庭均已传承四代，堪称养玉世家，父辈言传身教，二人耳濡目染，对玉之品德，倾心向往，深入其中，不能自拔，遂取"玉麟舍"为其雅号，以示其爱玉之心。一时间在京城收藏界，声名鹊起，影响日渐广泛。

交往日深，发现静麟、燕梅夫妇二人接人待物，颇多美玉风骨，在中国传统文化的洗礼中，在长达近二十年的艺术品收藏活动中，磨练了意志，升华了品质，以宽厚之心待人，交良友，敬师长，温良恭俭。二人举案齐眉，心有灵犀，行为举止，刚柔并济，钻研珍藏，日臻炉火纯青，而所涉猎收藏领域，更是不断延展，及杂项大成，领鼻烟壶风骚，亦收亦藏，游刃有余。

今日喜闻《心悦雅集》携春风而至，近百珍宝，尽藏其中。打开《心悦雅集》，或玉器、或烟壶、或杂项，扑面而来，皆为上品。主人的甜酸苦辣，汗水心血，饱含其中。仔细观之，或活灵活现，或耀眼夺目，或振聋发聩，确是精品云集，令人心悦。

感慨欣喜之余，作为多年好友，我有一句话与静麟、燕梅夫妇共勉：国之盛世，家道中兴，传统文化，触类旁通，潜心钻研，上下传承。愿你们在艺术品收藏领域心无旁骛，潜心钻研，收获更丰硕的成果。

《心悦雅集》，实在可喜可贺。

2011年7月8日

Preface

Zhang Rulan

When I first met Hei Jinglin and Ma Yanmei, I found them quite modest and a touch reserved. Yet the moment that the talk turned to jade, they suddenly grew very articulate and excited.

This loving couple, who possess a collection of many refined jade artworks, does not spring from powerful families, but their love for jade has been passed down over four generations. It may be apt to say that they come from a long line of jade aficionados. They have learned from their parents and from each other, and have developed an abiding interest in jade, enjoying a growing reputation among collectors in Beijing.

As I came to know the couple better, I discovered that the way they conducted themselves in relation to others shared the virtues ascribed to jade by Chinese people over the years. While collecting cultural objects over the last 20 years, they have tempered their spirit and refined their character. They treat people with consideration. They befriend good people and impart respect to elders and teachers. They are temperate, kind, courteous and restrained. This loving couple, who understand each other very well, has jointly researched the items in their collections. With a faultless knowledge of relevant articles, they have expanded their collection by adding snuff bottles and other antiques.

When I heard of the imminent publication of an album of nearly 100 valuable objects from Hei Jinglin's collection, I was most pleased. The jade work, snuff bottles and other antiques presented in the book are all fine pieces. They have been acquired by their owners through trial and tribulation. As you scrutinize them, they manifest themselves in vivid forms. Some of them impress you with their amazing beauty and others, with the profound cultural message inherent in them. Indeed, they are all true treasures.

Apart from my delight, as a long-standing friend, I would like to offer Hei Jinglin and Ma Yanmei some guidance: As the country is thriving, the family becomes prosperous too; traditional culture should be studied with focused attention and comprehended through analogy with related matters. I hope they will enhance their collection with continued dedication and achieve still greater success.

My warm congratulations on the publication of this album!

8 July 2011

序二

张广文

收藏的传统，古来有之：或是使用中收藏，一件物品，终其所用，转而收藏；或是有针对性地收藏有纪念意义的物品。人皆可收藏，人皆有收藏，但规模不同，选择不同，发展变化不同。宋以来至清，皇家收藏规模颇巨大，其中又多艺术珍品。明清两代，随着经济的发展，民间收藏兴起，出现了众多的收藏家，著名的收藏家大有人在，还有众多指导收藏的书籍。

相比较而言，在众多收藏品中，艺术珍品是少数的，有重大历史价值的藏品也是少量的。这些藏品的存在，表明了历史与艺术的真实及其存在，还给人们提供了欣赏、研究、了解、鉴别的机会。越是珍稀的藏品，它的公共性越强，越受社会的关注，且有较高的市场价值。

为社会提供了解藏品的机会，是博物馆和藏家的责任和义务。而举办藏品展示和出版藏品研究图册是重要的藏品表现方式。宋以前的文物收藏研究的书籍图册，目前见到的已经不多了。很多中国古代使用的器物，如指南针、地动仪，它们的形象、结构、性能如何，人们仅能推测。宋至清代，皇家、学者、藏家编写了多种书籍来介绍收藏物品，到今天这些书籍的价值依然存在。但是那时的图影制作水平、印刷水准尚未成熟，所保留下的影像准确性较差。时至今日，随着科学的发展，已经具备了准确传递影像的条件，大量收藏的作品被著录，被人们所了解、研究。这对于藏品及其收藏者、研究者非常必要，对促进收藏也非常有益。

众所周知，收藏者不但要重收藏，还要重鉴别，无鉴别知识的收藏家很难取得成功。文物及艺术品鉴赏很专业，也很难掌握，需要在收藏的过程中不断学习、总结、提高，自己有了认识、发现，要交流，要证明其科学，随时抛弃不科学的认知。通过收藏，由知之不多到知之甚多，由生手到里手再到高手，这是许多文物鉴赏者成长的过程。

当今收藏已成为时尚，很多人有收藏珍贵物品的能力及爱好。新藏家众多，同时市场上的劣质艺术品亦众多，以次充好，以新充旧的现象时有出现，这是收藏时所要注意的。

静麟夫妇的收藏进行了数十年，收藏多种古代文物及艺术精品，积累了丰富的鉴藏知识，是有成就的藏家。

静麟夫妇的收藏之所以能成功，在于其收藏方式。他们的收藏是有方向、有选择的收藏，瞄准几类藏品，又随缘而进，瓷、玉、象牙、烟壶、把件，几十年如一日，去粗取精，去伪取真，不断提高藏品的档次，重其质而增量，如沙里淘金、石里选玉，遴选出了精品。

相信静麟夫妇藏品的精选出版，对研究、收藏将大有裨益。

2011年7月

Preface II

Zhang Guangwen

Collecting rarities is a tradition. Some people collect things that they have used. Others purposefully collect commemorative objects. Anyone may become a collector, but collections vary in size and content. Collections grow and change in different ways. From the Song Dynasty (AD 960 ~ 1279) to 1911, imperial families possessed huge collections of various objects and the greater part of them were art treasures. From the Ming Dynasty (1368-1644), with development of the overall economy, private collectors emerged, many of whom had noted collections, with guidebooks also published for collectors.

Comparatively speaking, true gems of art make up a small part of all collections. Objects of great historical significance are rare. The existence of such objects in collections bears witness to history and artistic creativity. They offer opportunities for people to appreciate, study and evaluate ancient objects. The rarer the object, the more it belongs to the public and the greater attention it draws from society. At the same time, such objects would also have higher market value.

Collectors and museums have an obligation to inform the public about their collections. Exhibitions and publications are important ways to reveal such collections. Few books on the collection of cultural relics published prior to the Song Dynasty (AD 960 ~ 1279) survive today. As to the forms, structures and functions of many ingenious devices used in ancient China, such as the compass and seismograph, people today can only guess. From the Song to Qing dynasties (AD 960 ~ 1911), scholars, members of imperial families and private collectors compiled many books to introduce artefacts in their collections. Those books are still in existence. Yet the technology then used for making images and printing was not fully developed, so the images in such books are not accurate enough. Nowadays, with new methods to produce exact visual images, many collections have been more fully catalogued, and people can learn about and study the ancient objects gathered together. Publishing such books is very important for collectors, researchers and those who care for such a variety of collections, while also promoting collecting. The publication of Hei Jinglin's collection carries this significance.

As is known, collectors have to not only make efforts to acquire objects for their own collections, they must attach importance to the appraisal of their finds as well. A collector with little knowledge of valuation can hardly be successful. Connoisseurship of cultural relics and artworks is a challenging and difficult discipline. Collectors need to learn constantly, summing up their experiences from time to time and increasing their skills and knowledge through the actual collecting of objects. They must establish scientific views and discard unscientific views at all times. Through the collection of antiques, they acquire knowledge of many things which distinguishes them from those less informed persons, and which has turned them from beginners eventually to old hands, and then experts. Such is the process of growth of many appraisers of cultural objects.

Today, collecting cultural objects has come into vogue again. Many people have acquired an interest and expertise to collect rarities, and many new collectors have emerged. At the same time, poor artworks, fakes, forgeries, or newly made objects cloaked as antiques, are available in abundance. Collectors need to be careful.

Over the last decades, Hei Jinglin and his wife has gained a wealth of experience in the examining of antiques, which has been the crowning feature of his success.

Hei Jinglin and his wife collects antiques with clear goals, aimed at a few categories of specific objects, while at the same time, he also collects things that he comes across by chance. His collection spans ceramics, jade articles, ivory, snuff bottles, and small artifacts. Over the decades, he has made effective efforts to weed out fakes and retain the genuine, enhancing the value of his collection. Laying the emphasis on quality rather than quantity, he has selected a number of fine pieces from whatever he has come across. This method has been a contributing factor to his success.

Hei Jinglin and his wife are accomplished collectors of ancient objects and artworks. It is indeed welcome that the rarities in their collection are being published in a book.

July 2011

清代鼻烟壶概述

张荣　常自洁

鼻烟壶是盛放鼻烟的专用器具，是随着吸闻鼻烟习俗的兴起应运而生的。清代鼻烟壶的制作，首先从宫廷造办处开始，然后扩展到民间作坊。现存世的"康熙御制"款铜胎画珐琅鼻烟壶为清代最早、也是最为可信的御制鼻烟壶。由于清代康熙、雍正、乾隆皇帝对鼻烟壶的雅好和推崇，并将御制的鼻烟壶赐给远官近臣，鼻烟壶的制作，也由宫廷发展至民间，广东、扬州、苏州、北京、山东、景德镇、福州、内蒙古、宜兴等地先后竞相制作具有浓郁地方特色的鼻烟壶。地方官员为讨皇帝欢心，也将民间作坊制作的精美鼻烟壶贡入宫廷。清代鼻烟壶的制作呈现出官民并举，异彩纷呈的局面。

有清一代，用于制作鼻烟壶的材料很多，金、银、铜、瓷、玻璃、玉、松石、玛瑙、碧玺、水晶、翡翠、珊瑚、象牙、琥珀、蜜蜡、竹、木、葫芦、漆、紫砂、蚌壳、果核、铜胎珐琅等应有尽有，人们可根据各自所好，广泛选择。鼻烟壶的造型变化多端，除基本的背壶式外，还有人物、动物、植物等形状，惟妙维肖，不胜枚举。而鼻烟壶的纹饰，则题材广泛，丰富多彩，花鸟鱼虫、山水草木、亭台楼榭、珍禽瑞兽、人物故事、神话传说、吉祥图案等，大小不过掌中之物的鼻烟壶能集书法、绘画、雕刻、琢磨、烧造、镶嵌诸艺术之大成，是清代各种工艺美术繁荣和发展的缩影。到了晚清，还出现了鬼斧神工的内画鼻烟壶，为日渐衰落的晚清工艺，增添了一抹余晖。

鼻烟壶按其质地的不同大致可分为六类，即玻璃鼻烟壶、金属胎珐琅鼻烟壶、玉石鼻烟壶、瓷鼻烟壶、内画鼻烟壶、有机材质鼻烟壶。因篇幅所限，本文重点介绍玻璃、玉石、瓷三类鼻烟壶。

一　玻璃鼻烟壶

玻璃鼻烟壶以玻璃为材料，运用多种工艺手段制作而成。玻璃鼻烟壶在清代鼻烟壶中具有制作时间最早，延续时间最长，数量最多，工艺品种最为丰富等特点。从玻璃鼻烟壶的品种和加工工艺等方面，可以管窥整个清代玻璃制作的发展轨迹。清代烧造玻璃的产地主要有清宫造办处玻璃厂、山东博山、广州、扬州、北京等地。康熙三十五年（1696年），清宫玻璃厂成立，隶属于内务府造办处[①]。雍正年间，在圆明园又设立了分厂。据造办处档案记载，康熙朝已有黑色、绿色、白色、紫色、葡萄色、雨过天青等颜色的玻璃，但无鼻烟壶实物。雍正朝有单色玻璃、金星五彩玻璃、五彩缠丝玻璃、花玻璃、套玻璃、画珐琅玻璃鼻烟壶等；鼻烟壶的造型有八角形、鸡鼓式、油篓式等。乾隆朝玻璃鼻烟壶制作达到高峰，数量之多、品种之备、制作之精，令其他朝代难以企及。嘉庆以降，玻璃鼻烟壶数量骤减，生产技术下降，品种仅有单色玻璃。但玻璃鼻烟壶的制作，一直延续到宣统年间，未曾中断。按照清代玻璃工艺的分类原则与方法，玻璃鼻烟壶可以分为单色玻璃、套玻璃、画珐琅玻璃、金星玻璃、刻花玻璃、搅玻璃、描金玻璃、缠丝玻璃等。本文仅介绍套玻璃和画珐琅玻璃鼻烟壶。

套玻璃是康熙朝玻璃制作工艺的创新。所谓"套玻璃"是指由两种以上颜色玻璃制成的器物。其制作方法有两种，一是在玻璃胎上满套与胎色不同的另一色玻璃，之后在外层玻璃上雕琢花纹；一是用经加热半熔的色料棒直接在胎上作花纹。这两种方法制作出的器物均可现凸雕效果，既有玻璃的质色美，又有纹饰凹凸的立体美。套玻璃是玻璃成型工艺与雕刻工艺相结合的产物，是玻璃制作工艺史上的重要发明。清代著名学者赵之谦在光绪六年（1880年）编撰的《勇庐闲诘》中写到："时（康乾之时）天下大定，万物殷富，工执艺事，咸求修尚。于是列素点绚，以成文章，更创新制，谓之曰套。套者，白受彩也，先为之质曰地，则玻璃砗磲珍珠，其后尚明玻璃，微白，色若凝脂，或若霏雪，曰藕粉。套之色有红有蓝，更有兼套曰二彩、三彩、四彩、五彩或重叠套，雕镂精绝。康熙中所制浑朴简古，光照艳烂若异宝。乾隆以后，巧匠刻画，远过詹成，矩凿所至，细入毫发，扪之有棱……凡所造作或称曰皮，最著者曰辛家皮、勒家皮、袁家皮。"[②]遗憾的是，迄今尚未发现康熙朝的套玻璃器实物。雍正朝造办处档案中有制作套玻璃器及套玻璃鼻烟壶的记载，但未有实物流传下来。目前所见套玻璃仅有乾隆一朝的实物，既有套玻璃瓶、盘、炉等器物，也有套玻璃鼻烟壶。署有乾隆款的套玻璃鼻烟壶仅见单色套单色玻璃，如白套红、白套绿、白套蓝、红套蓝、绿套蓝等。而单色套多色玻璃鼻烟壶，传世量很大，水平不一，还未见署有官方年款的作品，过去一直认为是北京、扬州等民间作坊制作。故宫收藏一件乾隆款白套多色玻璃水丞，为清宫造办处玻璃厂所制。大量的单色套多色玻璃鼻烟壶是否有清宫玻璃厂的作品，还有待于研究。静麟夫妇所藏的9件套玻璃鼻烟壶均属于清代民间作品中之精品，有的造型秀美，如藕粉地套四色玻璃花蝶纹鼻烟壶，线条柔美，腹部扁平，是典型的清代中期鼻烟壶的造型；有的玻璃质感好，颜色纯正，如白套粉玻璃牧牛图鼻烟壶和白套绿玻璃梅花纹鼻烟壶，白色玻璃如温润的和田玉，粉色和绿色玻璃，色彩亮丽而柔和；有的花纹清晰，内容吉祥，如"官上加官"、"牧童放牛"、"松鹤延年"、"十里采荷"等；有的制作工艺复杂，如白套双色玻璃博古图鼻烟壶，采用的是双层套玻璃工艺，在清代套玻璃中比较少见。

玻璃胎画珐琅是清代首创的玻璃装饰工艺，始于康熙朝，由铜胎画珐琅发展而来。故宫博物院图书馆藏道光十五年（1835年）七月十一日立《珐琅玻璃宜兴瓷胎陈设档案》中有"康熙款玻璃胎珐琅牡丹蓝地胆瓶一件"的记载，是所见康熙朝画珐琅在官方汉文文献中的最早记录。台北故宫收藏的雍正款绿地竹叶纹鼻烟壶，是目前已知的最早的玻璃胎画珐琅鼻烟壶实物，见于雍正六年（1728年）的档案记载[3]。现存玻璃胎画珐琅以乾隆朝传世品相对较多。玻璃胎画珐琅是清代玻璃中制作工艺难度大，又具有较高艺术性的作品，它集玻璃、珐琅、绘画艺术于一身。玻璃胎画珐琅器的制作对生产技术要求较高，因玻璃与珐琅的熔点比较接近，温度低珐琅呈色不佳，温度高则玻璃易变形。从仅见的传世真品看，能够在寸天厘地的掌中珍玩内完整地表现出山水、人物和花鸟，确实体现了造办处匠师们鬼斧神工的

技艺。本书所收录的玻璃胎画珐琅开光西洋山水人物图鼻烟壶为个人收藏中之极品。玻璃胎画珐琅与清代盛行的铜胎、瓷胎、宜兴胎、金胎、银胎画珐琅相比，是制作难度最大，数量最少的一种，在清代即为皇家的重要收藏，被皇帝珍藏于乾清宫。其中玻璃胎胭脂水色画珐琅更是上品中之上品，北京故宫和台北故宫均无收藏。北京故宫仅藏一件铜胎画珐琅胭脂水色鼻烟壶。而静麟夫妇所藏的玻璃胎胭脂粉色画珐琅开光西洋山水人物图鼻烟壶实属难得，其装饰内容反映出乾隆时期西方文化对清朝皇室的影响。

正是由于玻璃胎画珐琅其独特魅力，故在晚清民间有"古月轩"之神秘传说，并有"古月轩"款瓷胎和玻璃胎画珐琅鼻烟壶传世。"古月轩"款鼻烟壶绝大部分为晚清民国之作。

二 玉石鼻烟壶

玉石鼻烟壶是鼻烟壶中的重要品种之一。清代制玉之地有宫内造办处玉作、苏州、扬州、南京、九江、杭州等地。其中造办处玉作、苏州、扬州的技术最为高超。康熙、雍正时期，造办处玉作制作的玉鼻烟壶数量较少，因清初新疆和田玉进贡受阻，直至乾隆二十四年（1759年），清政府平定了准噶尔叛乱后，恢复了中断一百多年的玉贡。每年春秋二季，新疆向宫廷贡玉四千斤，宫廷几乎垄断了新疆所产之玉。从一块璞玉，制作成一件令人赏心悦目的鼻烟壶，需经过选料、设计、画活、琢磨数道工序，兼采用浮雕、镂雕、阴刻、戗金等加工工艺。玉鼻烟壶以质地温润，造型变化多端，工艺精湛为其突出特点。仅其造型就有玉兰花、桃、石榴、柿子、葡萄、癞瓜等花果形，以及龟、鱼、蝉、蝙蝠、虎等吉祥动物造型。本书收录的玉质鼻烟壶可谓上乘之作，造型规矩，器形或小巧可爱，或端正饱满，玉质或细腻莹润、或纯净无瑕。装饰图案或喜庆，如"三狮戏球"、"喜报平安"，或具有文人韵味，如"渔樵耕读"、"四君子图"、"名人诗句"等，加工方法则量材施艺，或展现和田玉洁白无瑕的玉质感，如光素鼻烟壶；或采用巧雕，展

现玉的天然皮色，或在玉的表面镶嵌珊瑚、象牙等材料组成人物花鸟图案等。静麟夫妇所藏以上烟壶虽无款识，但应为清中期造办处玉作或苏州之作。

能够制作鼻烟壶的天然矿石除玉之外，其次是玛瑙，还有翡翠、芙蓉石、碧玺、青金石、孔雀石、绿松石、水晶、木变石等。本书收录的玛瑙鼻烟壶，均采用了俏色巧雕工艺，刻画出山石流水，花鸟人物，并配以李白、陶渊明诗句，具有浓郁的文人色彩，在玛瑙类鼻烟壶中独具一格。无色透明水晶鼻烟壶，纯净无杂质，晶莹剔透，造型秀美，周身雕刻团寿字，字体规整，令人爱不释手。

三　瓷鼻烟壶

江西景德镇是清代制瓷业的中心。清宫所需瓷鼻烟壶，由景德镇官窑烧造。乾隆年间，规定了御窑厂每年烧造50只鼻烟壶。官窑之外，景德镇民窑及其他地方的民窑也多有烧造鼻烟壶者。传世的康熙瓷鼻烟壶数量很少，造型多为爆竹筒式。雍正时期增加了四方、方形委角等器形，增烧了青花釉里红、茶叶末釉等品种，其色彩淡雅，釉色温润，装饰多以四季花卉、山水景致、婴戏等为题材。乾隆时期的御制瓷鼻烟壶最为精美，出现了葫芦式、灯笼式、扁方式、椭圆式、包袱式、花果式等千姿百态的造型；此时彩釉品种也大为增加，粉彩、五彩、墨彩、青花、窑变、金釉、仿松石、仿套玻璃、仿雕漆等相继出现，水平最高者仍是官窑粉彩。本书收录的"粉彩描金百子庆春图鼻烟壶"为乾隆朝官窑的典型之作。图案中共描绘了近百个童子，敲

锣、舞龙、放鞭炮，牵象、举鱼、吹喇叭，好一派热闹场景，孩童个个喜笑颜开，兴高采烈，让人看后忍俊不禁。百子图是清代皇家喜用的装饰图案，在雕漆、瓷器中经常使用，它反映了统治者的美好愿望，希望子孙兴旺，江山永固。但在方寸之间的鼻烟壶上描绘百子形象，可谓鬼斧神工。

四　结语

鼻烟壶在清代的广泛盛行，一方面与其制作精巧有关，另一方面与统治者的嗜好、推崇分不开。拥有鼻烟壶数量的多少，曾是身份、地位和荣耀的象征。清代鼻烟壶的制作，从早期的精细到晚期的粗糙，也映射出大清王朝由盛到衰的历史轨迹。如今，世界各地都有不少鼻烟壶的收藏者和爱好者，鼻烟壶已成为人们欣赏、把玩、收藏的艺术珍品。

看静麟夫妇的收藏就能看到他们的学识和修养。他们的收藏不仅品类齐全，而且上品云集，百看不厌。除鼻烟壶外，其他杂项的收藏也同样是品类上乘，佳作频出。众多藏品从材质上讲包括金、银、玉、陶瓷、玻璃、翡翠、芙蓉石、水晶、玛瑙、雕漆、象牙、犀角、琥珀、蜜蜡、珍珠、紫檀、沉香等近20余种，丰富多彩，美不胜收。从使用功能上看，有文房清供日常陈设品、佩饰、手把件、鼻烟壶等。通过他们无不透出收藏者广博的知识，独到的审美和大家的风范。

在编辑本书的过程中考虑到读者的一般习惯，我们将静麟夫妇丰富的藏品分为三部分，即玉器、鼻烟壶和杂项。虽然没有完全按照时代、材质或使用功能分类排序，但这种分类排序方式是为了让读者相对集中地了解一类或一种文物，希望读者能够接受和喜欢。

注释：
①《钦定大清会典事例》卷千一百七十三，"养心殿造办处"条。
②《勇庐闲诘》，《丛书集成新编》卷四七，页765，新文丰出版公司。
③《造办处各作成做活计清档》胶片65号，中国第一历史档案馆。

Snuff Bottles Produced During the Qing Dynasty

Zhang Rong   Chang Zijie

Bottles to hold snuff (powdered tobacco) came into being with the popularity of inhaling snuff. Manufacture of snuff bottles began in the Palace Workshop during the Qing Dynasty, and later expanded to privately workshops. An extant bronze snuff bottle with enamel coating and the inscription, "Made in the imperial kiln during Kangxi reign," is the earliest and most authentic snuff bottle made in the court. Thanks to emperors Kangxi, Yongzheng and Qianlong, who reigned from 1662 to 1795 and had a passion for snuff bottles, often granting them to their subordinates, these bottles found their way from court craftsmen to common artisans, as in Guangdong Province, Yangzhou, Suzhou and Yixing in Jiangsu Province, Beijing, Shandong, Jingdezhen in Jiangxi Province, Fuzhou in Fujian Province, present-day Inner Mongolia, and other regions. To carry favor from the emperor, local officials used to pay tribute offering fine snuff bottles to the court. During the Qing Dynasty, snuff bottles produced both in the court and in private workshops displayed a diverse beauty.

During the Qing Dynasty, various materials were used to produce snuff bottles. Those materials included gold, silver, copper, porcelain, glass, jade, turquoise, agate, crystal, emerald, coral, ivory, amber, bamboo, wood, calabash, lacquer, *Zisha*, shells, fruit seeds or pits, and enamel. There was a large variety catering to different tastes. The shapes of snuff bottles also greatly increased. Apart from the basic shape of the upright flat circular bottle, snuff bottles were crafted in the shape of human figures, animals, plants, and other objects. Decorations of the snuff bottle included flowers, insects, birds, landscape, houses, animals, anecdotes, mythical stories, and auspicious designs. Small enough to be held in the palm, snuff bottles synthesizing the best of calligraphy, painting, engraving, polishing, firing and embedding, epitomized the various branches of the handicraft industry of that time. By the latter phases of the dynasty, the emergence of the inside-painted snuff bottle added brilliance to a declining handicraft industry. In terms of materials used, snuff bottles are categorized into the glass snuff bottle, metal snuff bottle with enamel coating, jade snuff bottle, porcelain snuff bottle, inside-painted snuff bottle, and snuff bottles made of organic materials. Limited space allows the introduction only of glass, jade and porcelain snuff bottles.

I. Glass Snuff Bottle

The glass snuff bottle was produced by various methods. Among snuff bottles made during the Qing Dynasty, glass ones emerged the earliest, lasted the longest time, and were produced in the largest quantities and the largest number of varieties. The varieties and processing methods of glass snuff bottles also trace the development of glassmaking through the Qing Dynasty. The main producers of glass were the glass works under the Palace Workshop, and workshops in Boshan, Shandong Province, Guangzhou, Yangzhou and Beijing. Glasswork under the Palace Workshop was established in 1696. An affiliate workshop was set up in the capital's Yuanmingyuan Garden during the reign of Yongzheng (r. 1722~1735). According to files from the Palace Workshop, during the reign of Kangxi (1661~1722), glass in black, green, white, purple, azure and other colours were produced, but no snuff bottles of that time have survived. During the ensuing reign of Yongzheng, snuff bottles were made of plain glass, multicolour glass with golden stars, colour glass, fine-veined multicoloured glass, layered glass and enamel-coated glass, in the shapes of octagons, drums and traditional oil baskets. During the reign of Qianlong (1736~1795), the manufacture of glass snuff bottles reached a height that no other period of time has ever reached in terms of output, variety and level of craftsmanship. After that period, production of snuff bottles declined both in output and in workmanship. Since then only monochrome glass was used to make snuff bottles. But manufacture of glass snuff bottles continued until 1911. According to technical specifications for glass produced during the Qing Dynasty, glass snuff bottles are classified into such types as monochrome glass, layered glass, enamel-coated glass, glass with golden stars, glass with engraved designs, glass with gold-lined designs, and glass with attached designs of fine or broad glass strands. In this article, only snuff bottles made of layered glass and glass with an enamel coating will be introduced.

Layered glass was an innovation during the reign of Kangxi. A layered glass object was produced with glass of two or more colours. There were two methods to produce such glassware. One was to cover the roughcast of a glass object with another layer of glass of a different colour and to carve designs on the outer layer of glass. The other method was to apply designs with a half-melted strand of heated glass of another colour to the surface of glass roughcast. Objects made using either of the above-mentioned methods have designs in relief, while at the same time retaining the material appeal of the glass. As a combination of casting and cutting, layered glass was a major innovation in glassmaking. In 1880, the famous scholar Zhao Zhiqian wrote, "During the reigns of Kangxi and Qianlong the whole country was a peace and production abound. Workers and artisans all pursued perfection in their work. They added ornamentation to plain objects and put out new varieties of their products by attaching designs on them. This work was called 'ply ware.' 'Ply' means a coloured design on a plain background. First, they produced roughcast using glass, giant clams or pearls, and later, roughcast was made of translucent glass in white grey or rose colours. The layer of glass attached to the roughcast was red or blue. Sometimes, two, three, four or five colours were applied in one or several layers. The carving of the glass was exquisite. Such objects produced during the reign of Kangxi were in simple form but shone like gems. Starting from the reign of Qianlong, skilled artisans painted or carved on them using lines as fine as hair. One can feel the raised parts. All such decorations were called coatings, the best-known being Xin's, Le's and Yuan's coatings." Unfortunately, up to date no layered glass objects from the Kangxi Reign have been recovered. Files of the

Palace Workshop of the Yongzheng Reign have been discovered recording manufacture of layered glass snuff bottles and other objects, but no real objects have survived. Surviving layered glass objects are all from Qianlong's reign, including bottles, plates, incense burners and snuff bottles. Snuff bottles with the inscription "Qianlong Reign" were all made by applying glass of one colour to plain roughcast, such as red, green or blue coatings on white roughcast, or a blue coating on red or green roughcast.

Snuff bottles with monochrome roughcast and multicolour coatings have survived in large number but they show different levels of craftsmanship. None of them bear an official inscription. In the past, researchers believed that such snuff bottles had been produced by private-run workshops in Beijing and Yangzhou. But the collection of the Palace Museum, includes a glass water vessel made of a white body with a multicolour coating that had been produced in the glassworks under the Palace Workshop. Whether most of the snuff bottles with a multicolour coating on monochrome roughcast were produced in the glassworks under the Palace Workshop remains a question to be answered by researchers. The nine layered glass snuff bottles in Hei Jinglin and his wife's collection are fine works from the Qing-dynasty's privately run workshops. Some have beautiful forms, like the rose snuff bottle with designs of flowers and butterflies in four colours. The upright flat bottle with design in fine and slender lines is a typical piece dating to the middle part of the Qing Dynasty. Some of them set off the beautiful colours of the glass, like the white snuff bottle with red designs of a cowherd, and the white snuff bottle with designs of green plum blossoms. The white glass in those bottles is like the smooth and fine jade from Khotan, and the red and green glass are soft and brilliant. Some of his snuff bottles have distinct cutting, and bear auspicious designs such as those symbolizing repeated promotions in rank, and images of cowherds, cranes and pines and lotus flowers gatherers. Some of his bottles are noted for their technical sophistication, like the snuff bottle with designs of antiques, which was made of two layers of glass. This is a rare Qing-dynasty two-layer glass artefact.

Coating glass roughcast with enamel was a new technique created during the Kangxi Reign. Its precursor was enamelled bronzeware. The library of the Palace Museum has a record of "a blue glass bottle with a painted enamel coating," in the file "Glass Objects with Enamel Coating for Display Produced in Yixing," dated on the eleventh day of the seventh lunar month, 1835. This is the earliest Chinese-language record on enamel coating of the Kangxi era. A snuff bottle, with designs of green bamboo leaves and the inscription "made during the Yongzheng Reign," is the earliest glass snuff bottle with enamel coating confirmed so far. It is recorded in a file put together in 1728. Most extant enamelled glass snuff bottles are products of the Qianlong reign. Technically speaking, manufacture of such snuff bottles was rather difficult, but they possess higher artistic value. They were a synthesis of glassmaking, enamel processing, and painting.

Making such bottles involved exacting skills, because the melting points of glass and enamel are close. If the temperature in the kiln was too low, the fired enamel would show faint colour; and if the temperature was too high, the glass bottle would deform. Judging from the decoration on surviving snuff bottles, landscape, human figures, birds and flowers presented within the space of a square inch exhibit the superlative craftsmanship of the artisans who produced the bottles. A glass snuff bottle with a European landscape painted with enamel, and the inscription "made during the reign of Qianlong," is a masterpiece that any collector could have found. Compared to enamelled bronze, porcelain, gold, silver and earthenware bottles prevalent during the Qing Dynasty, producing glass bottles with enamel coating required the highest level of difficulty, and therefore output was the smallest. Such bottles were stored in the Palace of Heavenly Purity of the imperial palace. The glass bottle with a rose enamel coating is the finest among the fine pieces, but it is not to be found either in the Palace Museum in Beijing or the Palace Museum in Taipei. The Palace Museum in Beijing has only one bronze snuff bottle painted with rose enamel. The theme of the decoration on this glass snuff bottle in Hei Jinglin and his wife's collection reflects the influence of European culture on the Qing court during the reign of Qianlong.

It is due to the special charm of the enamelled glass bottle that a mysterious legend about the "Gu Yue Studio," an alleged manufacturer of such bottles, has passed down through oral tradition. The legend has inspired the manufacture of porcelain bottles and glass bottles with the inscription "Gu Yue Studio." Those bottles were largely produced during the end of the Qing Dynasty or the beginning of the Republic of China.

II. Jade Snuff Bottle

Jade bottles represent an important variety of the snuff bottle. During the Qing Dynasty, jade articles were produced at the Jade Works under the Palace Workshop, and at other jade workshops in Suzhou, Yangzhou, Nanjing, Jiujiang and Hangzhou. Of those jade workshops, those under the Palace Workshop and those in Suzhou and Yangzhou had the most sophisticated technology. Because jade tributes from Khotan, Xinjiang, were hindered during the early phase of the Qing Dynasty, the jade works under the Palace Workshop produced only a small number of jade snuff bottles during the Kangxi and Yongzheng reigns. Not until the Qing government put down the Jungar Rebellion in 1756, were jade tributes from Khotan resumed to the court, after a hiatus of 100 years. From then on, 200 kilograms of jade were paid to the court in spring and autumn every year. The Qing court had a monopoly on the fine jade from Xinjiang. From a block of unpolished jade to an eye-pleasing snuff bottle, artisans went through the process of selecting jade, designing, outlining, polishing, carving, drilling, engraving, gilding, etc. Jade snuff bottles are noted for their smooth and fine material, diverse shapes and consummate craft. In terms of form, jade snuff bottles take on shapes of magnolia, peach, pomegranate, persimmon, grape, gourd, tortoise, fish, cicada, bat, tiger, and many others. The snuff bottles presented in this book are all fine works. They are small but of lovely form, and the jade used is crystal and smooth. Decorations on them are either auspicious designs (e.g. three lions playing with a ball, magpies bearing good news) or designs with literary messages (e. g. fishing, woodcutting, cultivating and reading, the four "gentlemen" plants – pine, bamboo, plum and orchid, and verses from famous poets). Those bottles were processed in different ways. Some are plain, so as to set off the superb quality of the white and clean jade from Khotan. Others are ingeniously carved, so as to show off the natural colour of the unpolished part of the jade. Still others are embedded with coral, ivory and other precious material to form designs of human figures, birds and flowers. Though these snuff bottles bear no inscriptions, their superlative craftsmanship convincingly pinpoints their manufacture to jade works in the court or in Suzhou.

Apart from jade, natural minerals like agate, emerald, rose quartz, tourmaline, lazurite, malachite, turquoise, crystal and petrified wood are also used to make snuff bottles. The agate snuff bottles presented in this book are skilfully carved to expose part of the unpolished surface of the agate and display rocks, water, birds, flowers and human figures with inscriptions of lines from the great poets Tao Yuanming and Li Bai. A crystal snuff bottle in the book bears the circularized characters *Shou*

(longevity) on its body. It is transparent and clearly processed with amazing dexterity.

III. Porcelain Snuff Bottle

Jingdezhen in Jiangxi Province was the centre of production for ceramics during the Qing Dynasty. Porcelain snuff bottled used in the Qing court were made in government-run kilns in Jingdezhen. During the Qianlong Reign (1736~1795), the production quota at imperial kilns was 50 snuff bottles a year. Apart from government-run kilns, privately run kilns produced snuff bottles too. Few snuff bottles produced during the Kangxi Reign have survived, and they are mostly those shaped as upright cylinders. During the reign of Yongzheng (1722~1735), square and round-cornered oblong snuff bottles were produced and new varieties of blue-and-white snuff bottles with red designs under glaze, and bronze-coloured snuff bottles also emerged. Such bottles glazed in subtle and delighting hues were decorated with designs of flowers from all seasons, landscapes and children. Snuff bottles produced during the Qianlong reign were the most beautiful. New varieties took on the shape of a calabash, a lantern, fruit, flowers or a bundle, and some of them were in oval or upright flat and oblong shapes. Decorating them was greatly diversified with emergence of famille rose, five-coloured, blue-and-white and golden glazed snuff bottles, snuff bottles with black designs on them, bottles covered with glaze that had undergone transmutation during firing, and bottles in style of turquoise, layered glass and carved lacquerware. The best snuff bottles were produced in government-run kilns. The "Famille Rose Snuff Bottle with Painting of 100 Children Celebrating Spring," pictured in this book, is a typical product from a government-run kiln of the Qianlong era. The picture on the bottle shows nearly 100 children playing gongs and trumpets, dancing the dragon dance, lighting crackers, leading an elephant and holding fish midst a jubilant atmosphere. The depiction of 100 children was a favourite theme for decoration of imperial artefacts including carved lacquerware and porcelain during the Qing Dynasty. The theme reflected the rulers' wishes for a flourishing family line and eternal order in the country. Yet the imagery of 100 children presented within the space of one inch does exhibit tremendous craft.

IV. Conclusion

The popularity snuff bottles enjoyed during the Qing Dynasty was attributed to the exquisite workmanship they displayed and at the same time, to the taste and patronage of rulers. The number of snuff bottles in a person's possession was once a sign of a person's status. The evolution of snuff bottles from being exquisitely produced to being crudely made went hand in hand with the decline of the dynasty. Today many collectors and lovers of snuff bottles are found everywhere in the world. The snuff bottle has become an artistic treasure viewed, enjoyed and collected by people.

A person's collection reflects his learning and personal character. Hei Jinglin and his wife does not have a collection of all types of antiques, but he boasts a great number of fine artworks. Apart from snuff bottles, the other objects in his collection are all of good quality. The collections can be divided into objects for the scholar's studio, ornaments, jewellery and hand pieces, and are made of gold, silver, jade, porcelain, glass, jadeite, ross quartz, crystal, agate, carving lacquer, ivory, rhinoceros horn, amber, pearl, redsandalwood and aloewood and so on. All of the collections underlie a connoisseur's extensive knowledge and unique eye for beauty.

In consideration of reading habit, we put the collections into three parts: jades, snuff bottles and other antiques. In order to understand the artworks in a better way, the book didn't use the method of classification according to date, material or application, and hope for your receiving and understanding.

图版 Plates

玉器篇 Jade

玉鸠

宋
高 3.9厘米　长 7.3厘米

　　旧玉，沁色以黑色为主，包浆自然。鸠呈卧姿，展翅，体较扁。圆头，圆眼，短颈，喙短且尖，左右眼睛以朱砂填色，呈红色。颈后有三层平行的细密阴刻线，翅左右及尾尖也均以阴线刻划，简洁明快。

　　玉鸠主要见于汉代，多用于装饰杖首。《后汉书·礼仪》有关于用鸠的记载："仲秋之月，县道皆案户比民。年始七十者，授之以王杖，铺之糜粥。八十九十，礼有加赐。王杖长（九）尺，端以鸠鸟为饰。鸠者，不噎之鸟也。欲老人不噎。是月也，祀老人星于国都南郊老人庙。"可见自古以来鸠就有代表长生不老的文化含义。此件玉鸠为仿汉代作品，古朴自然，让人爱不释手。

Jade turtledove

Song Dynasty (AD960~1279)
Height 3.9cm　　Length 7.3cm

　　The bird is sculpted from ancient jade that has black traces of oozing, and a natural luster. The reclining bird has its wings spread out. It has round eyes, short beak, short neck and round head. Its eyes are colored with cinnabar. Behind its neck are three parallel incised lines. The tips of its wings are also incised concisely.

　　The jade turtledove was popular during the Han Dynasty (206 BC ~ AD 220), usually ornamenting the top of walking sticks. The chapter on "Rites," in *History of Latter Han*, records: "In the second month of the autumn, county and circuit magistrates inspected the local people from household to household. People above the age of 70 were granted a walking stick and meat porridge. Those older than 80 or 90 were given an even better gift. The walking stick as a gift from the lord is nine chi long, on top of which is carved a turtledove. The turtledove is a bird that never chokes on food. The gift expresses a wish that old people will never choke on their food. In this month, people make offerings to the Old Man Star in the Old Man's Temple to the south of the capital." Since ancient times, the turtledove had a connotation of longevity. A copy of a Han-dynasty product, this jade turtledove is lovely in its simple appearance.

玉鸡形坠

宋
高 2.1厘米　长 3.5厘米

　　旧玉，玉质油润。圆雕，鸡呈伏卧状，琢云头形鸡冠，圆眼尖喙，颈部粗短，并有一圈短阴刻线示羽毛，短阴刻线下有一圈凸起的棱线，上饰一周阴刻的波折纹。长尾拱起后下弯，翅膀和尾部用长阴线刻划出羽毛。双爪收于腹下。鸡背有一上下贯通的方孔，用以系佩。玉鸡造型丰满圆润，线条简单流畅，雕工简洁写实。

Jade pendant in the shape of a chicken

Song Dynasty (AD960~1279)
Height 2.1cm　Length 3.5cm

　　This round sculpture of a chicken is carved from a piece of fine and smooth ancient jade. The chicken with a cloud-shaped crest, round eyes and a sharp beak sits prone. A ring of short incised lines on its neck suggest feathers, and beneath the short lines is a raised ring with an incised wavy line on it. Its long tail is raised high before droping down, and long feathers are engraved on its wings and tail. Its claws are drawn under its belly. On its back is a square hole for stringing. The plump chicken sculpted with concise and fluent lines is quite naturalistic.

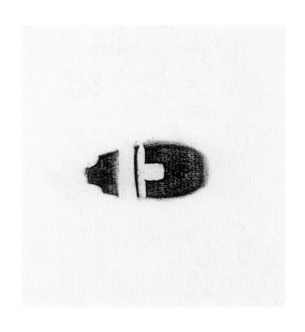

白玉山水人物纹瓃子

宋
高 5.9厘米　径 1.3厘米

　　白玉质，玉质细腻温润。瓃子呈两头细中间略粗的圆柱状，上下有通天孔。器身上有线刻山水人物纹，在方寸间竟刻划出11个人物，似一幅山水人物画卷，两只小船行于山水间，船上各有3人，岸边松树下有人驻足观望，也有两人似在对弈。线条虽细若游丝，却如行云流水般流畅，显示出工匠高超的雕琢技艺。

　　玉瓃子源于史前时期的玉管饰，一般都有通天孔，可单独佩戴使用，其制作使用一直延续到明清时期，形成了一个器形丰富，纹饰多样的瓃子系列。

White jade *Lezi* tube with design of landscape and human figures

Song Dynasty (AD960~1279)
Height 5.9cm　Diameter 1.3cm

　　The *Lezi* is a tube with thinner ends, and hollow for threading. The wall of the tube, covering no more than 10 square centimeters, has an incised landscape with 11 human figures. Two boats are meandering on the river, and each boat has three human figures in it. On one bank, a man is watching, and two men are playing chess. The lines are as slim as gossamer yet fluently executed, revealing the superb skill of the creator of the tube.

　　Originating in prehistoric times, the *Lezi* is usually hollow throughout. It can be worn alone. The making of *Lezi* continued until the early 20th century. Owing to this history, there are still found rich varieties of *Lezi* with sundry decorations.

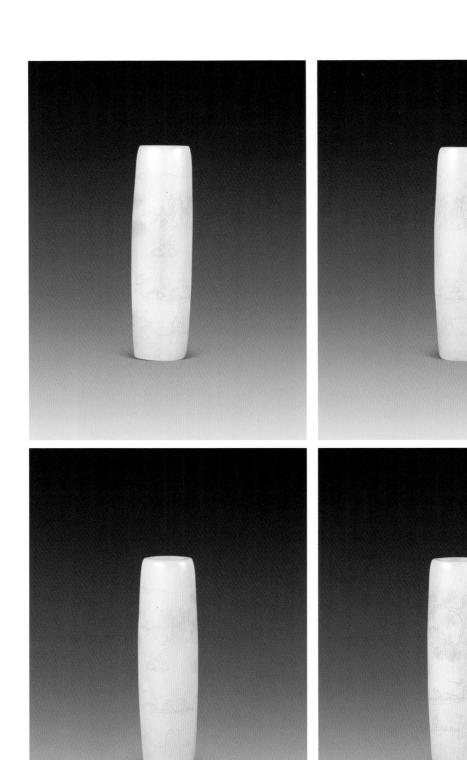

青白玉秋葵绶带鸟纹饰件

金
长 8.1厘米　宽 5.6厘米

　　青白玉质，饰件呈椭圆形，正面微凸。采用多层镂雕工艺雕琢一绶带鸟展翅回首立于秋葵花叶丛中，嘴啄羽毛。花叶舒展，叶脉清晰，叶片上利用玉皮颜色俏色点缀。叶脉、鸟羽皆用阴刻线表示。此件器物的雕琢技法具有宋代多层镂雕技法的风格，层次感强。

Greenish-white jade ornament with design of paradise flycatcher and okra

Jin Dynasty (1115~1234)
Length 8.1cm　Width 5.6cm

　　The sculpture is oval shaped with its front raised slightly. A fretted paradise flycatcher stands among the flowers with its head turning back and its wings fanning out. It is preening its feathers with its beak. The veins of the leaves are clearly incised. The leaves have spots on them, which are part of the jade's color. The birds' feathers are presented in incised lines. Technically, this sculpture is produced by fretting several distinct layers, a method widely employed during the Song Dynasty (AD960~1279).

青白玉柞树双猴纹饰件

元
长 8.4厘米　宽 4.4厘米

　　青白玉质，呈不规则的长方形，采用镂雕工艺雕琢山石、柞树、双猴等画面，风格写实。利用皮色巧雕为树叶，以阴刻线示叶脉，山石的孔洞有的镂空，有的只是用实心钻点挖而成的小圆坑来表示。单面工，背面有因镂雕留下的孔洞。此件器物从题材和构图形式上也可属秋山玉的范畴，充满了山林野趣。其雕琢手法具有比较明显的元代玉器粗犷豪放的风格。

Greenish-white jade ornament with design of two monkeys on an oak

Yuan Dynasty (1279~1368)
Length 8.4cm　Width 4.4cm

　　This uneven rectangular piece of jade has open carvings of rocks, an oak and two monkeys in a realistic style. The surface of the jade lends its color to leaves, and the veins on leaves are presented in incised lines. The caves in the mountain are represented by holes, while small caves are presented through shallow cavities on its surface. All the images are on one side, while the other side has holes left over from the cutting. The sculpture exhibits the charm of a mountain in autumn. The cutting techniques employed partake of the bold and rough style of Yuan-dynasty jade work.

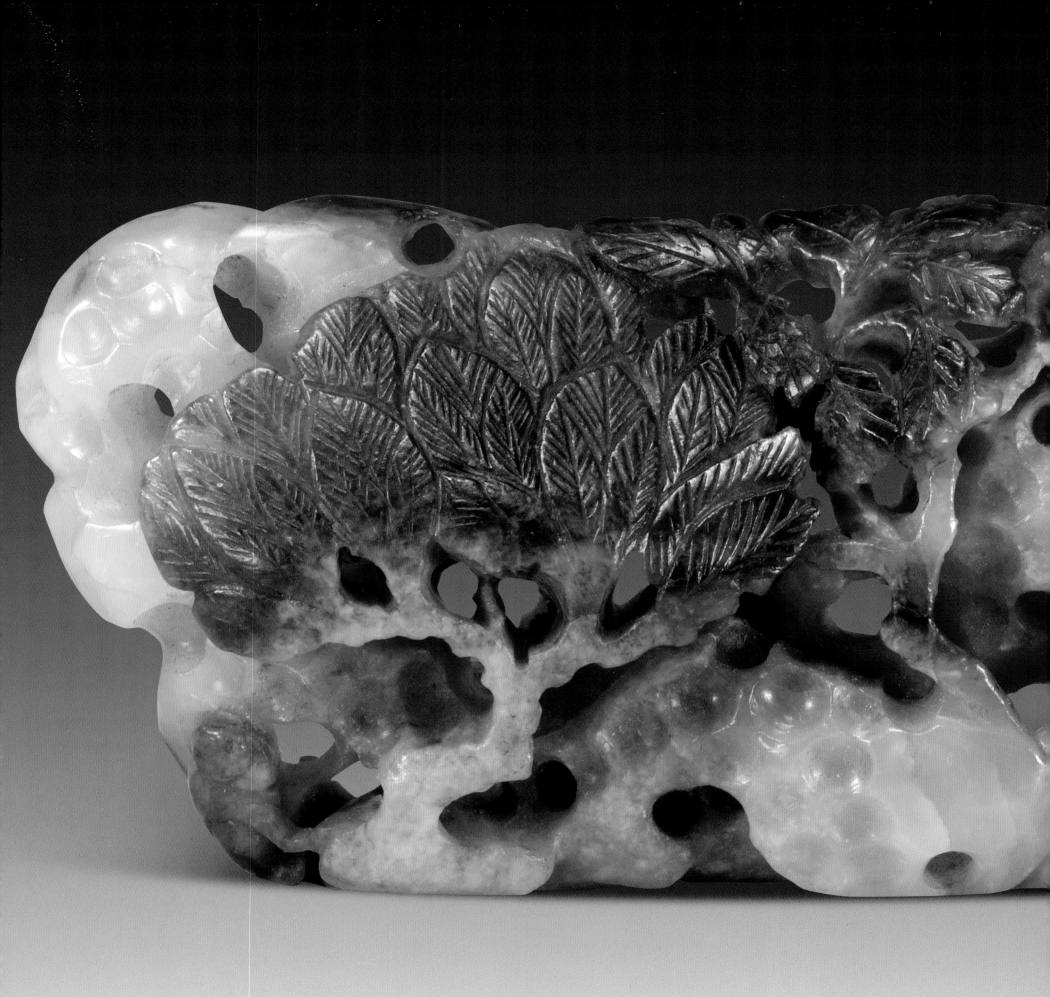

白玉抱鹅童子形坠

明
高 5.9厘米　宽 3.1厘米

　　白玉质带糖色，玉质油润。圆雕，童子站立状，一脚前，一脚后。头梳单髻，圆脸，长圆形眼睛，大鼻子，嘴角上翘呈微笑状。身着右衽窄袖长袍，腰系宽带，飘垂于下，脚着云头鞋。左手抱一拨楞鼓，右手抱鹅。鹅卧姿，头埋在身体里，尾巴上翘。自头顶至足下有通天孔，可供穿缀。雕琢风格自然写实。

White jade pendant in the shape of child holding a goose

Ming Dynasty (1368~1644)
Height 5.9cm　Width 3.1cm

　　The pendant is made of an oily and brownish white jade. The sculpted child stands, one foot in front. He has a bun of hair on his head. His round face has large oval eyes, a high nose, and a smiling mouth. He wears a long robe with its large front buttoned to the right. A wide sash at the waist has hanging ends. On his feet are shoes with designs of clouds on them. He holds a rattle drum in his left hand, and in his right hand, a goose whose head is buried in its body with its tail raised. A hole through the pendant, from top to the bottom, enables stringing. The sculpture is in a naturalistic style.

白玉持荷童子形坠

明
高 4.7厘米　宽 4.2厘米

　　白玉质，局部有皮色。以一块籽料随形圆雕而成。童子屈膝作蹲姿，大眼圆睁，面带笑容，头梳双髻，憨态可掬。左手在胸前，右手于头侧，共握一枝大莲茎，莲茎从右侧绕过后背垂于左下方。童子造型写实，手法简洁明快，神态活泼可爱。细部运用传统的阴刻手法，琢刻线条自然流畅。

　　玉雕"持荷童子"最早出现于宋代，也是两宋玉器中最为流行的玉雕题材，并延续至明清，具有浓厚的生活气息。其形象源于"鹿母生莲"这一佛教故事，成人佩戴寓意"连生贵子"，孩子佩戴则寓意"健康成材"。

White jade in the shape of child holding a lotus

Ming Dynasty (1368~1644)
Height 4.7cm　Width 4.2cm

　　This round sculpture is carved from a nugget of jade with some surfaces unpolished. The smiling child is squatting, and has round eyes and two hair buns on his head. He holds a large lotus flower, with his left hand in front of his chest, and his right hand at his head. The stem of the lotus extends around his right side down to the left behind him. This lively and lovely child is realistically and concisely sculpted. Details are executed with smooth incising lines, which is a traditional technique.

　　Jade sculpture with this theme became popular during the Song Dynasty (AD960~1279), and remained popular through ensuing dynasties until the early 20th century. The theme derives from a Buddhist tale about a deer giving birth to a lotus. For adult wearers, the pendant implies future noble offspring, and for children, it symbolizes healthy growth.

8

白玉鹘捕天鹅饰件

明
长 7.8厘米　宽 5.5厘米

　　白玉质，采用分层镂雕工艺雕琢鹘捕天鹅的画面。正面微呈弧凸，以荷莲茨菰为地，琢一天鹅展翅，长喙微张，伸颈从一支菰茎下钻出。左上方一身形娇小的鹘立于荷叶之上，圆眼尖喙，振翅回望，似在寻找天鹅的踪迹。鹘和天鹅的翅膀和尾羽均以阴刻线表示。

　　放鹘捕鹅为辽代春捺钵的主要活动，从而也衍生出以此为题材的一类别具民族特色的玉雕作品——春水玉，并从辽金一直延续到明清时期，图案渐趋简单化，从鹘鹅之间的激烈搏斗到两者之间相安无事，寓意也由表现游牧民族的粗犷豪放转为祥和宁静。

White jade ornament with design of a falcon catching a swan

Ming Dynasty (1368~1644)
Length 7.8cm　Width 5.5cm

　　The object is pierced and carved out into several layers, representing a falcon capturing a swan. The obverse is slightly raised, showing a swan with its beak open flying from under a stem of wild rice. On the top left, a falcon stands on a lotus leaf, with round eyes and sharp beak, flapping its wings and turning its head around, as if gazing at the swan. The wings of the falcon and swan are all incised with lines.

　　Releasing falcons to catch geese in the spring was a major event for the imperial family during the Liao Dynasty (AD907~1125) and this gave rise to jade carvings on the theme of this nationality. From the Liao Dynasty to the Qing Dynasty, the representation of such themes became simplified – from a fierce struggle between the two birds to peaceful coexistence, an evolution in parallel with the nomadic people's shift from being a warrior clan to becoming a peace-loving people.

9

白玉麒麟绶带鸟摆件

明
高 10.3厘米　长 14.5厘米

　　白玉质，玉色白中闪青。麒麟作蹲卧回首状，双眼圆睁，翘鼻，嘴齐平，张口露齿，尖耳长角，牛蹄形足，狮形尾，长尾弯折。身饰鳞纹，并用细阴刻线刻划毛发。麒麟口衔飘带，带系一书，有麒麟吐书之意。绶带鸟回首，口衔灵芝。胸俯落于地，首上抬，细长眼，尖喙，头有长冠，长尾飘于身后，尾端下垂内卷，身饰羽纹。麒麟与绶带首尾相接，前后呼应，共同立于玉台之上。此摆件体量较大，高低错落有致。麒麟和绶带鸟自古以来就被视为祥瑞，象征着吉祥长寿。

White jade sculpture with design of *Qilin* and paradise flycatcher

Ming Dynasty (1368~1644)
Height 10.3cm　Length 14.5cm

　　A mythical creature, the *qilin*, is sculpted in pale greenish white jade, seated with its head turned around, showing wide-open eyes, a snub snout, flush lips, bared teeth, sharp ears, long horns, feet with a bull's hooves, and a lion's fanning tail. Its body is incised with designs of scales and fine hair. The creature holds a ribbon in its mouth, with a book tied to the ribbon. A paradise flycatcher, with the mythical glossy ganoderma herb in its beak, turns its head to the creature and presses its breast to the ground. The bird has narrow eyes, a sharp beak, a high crest over its head, and a long tail rising and falling on its back. Its body has designs of feathers. The creature's head touches the bird's tail. The *Qilin*, has been regarded as an auspicious sign, and the bird's name in Chinese, *Shoudai*, is partly homonymous with the word for longevity (*Shou*), hence a symbol for a long life.

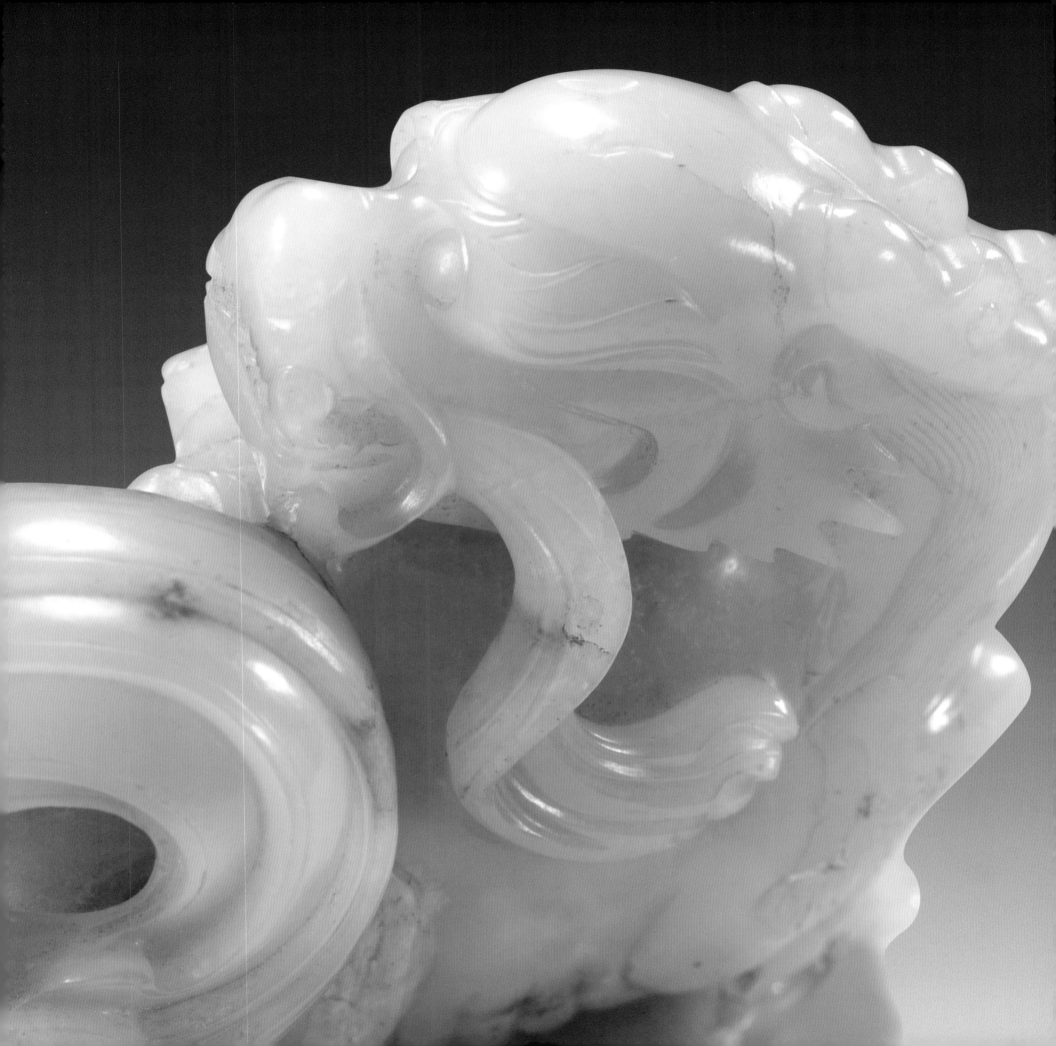

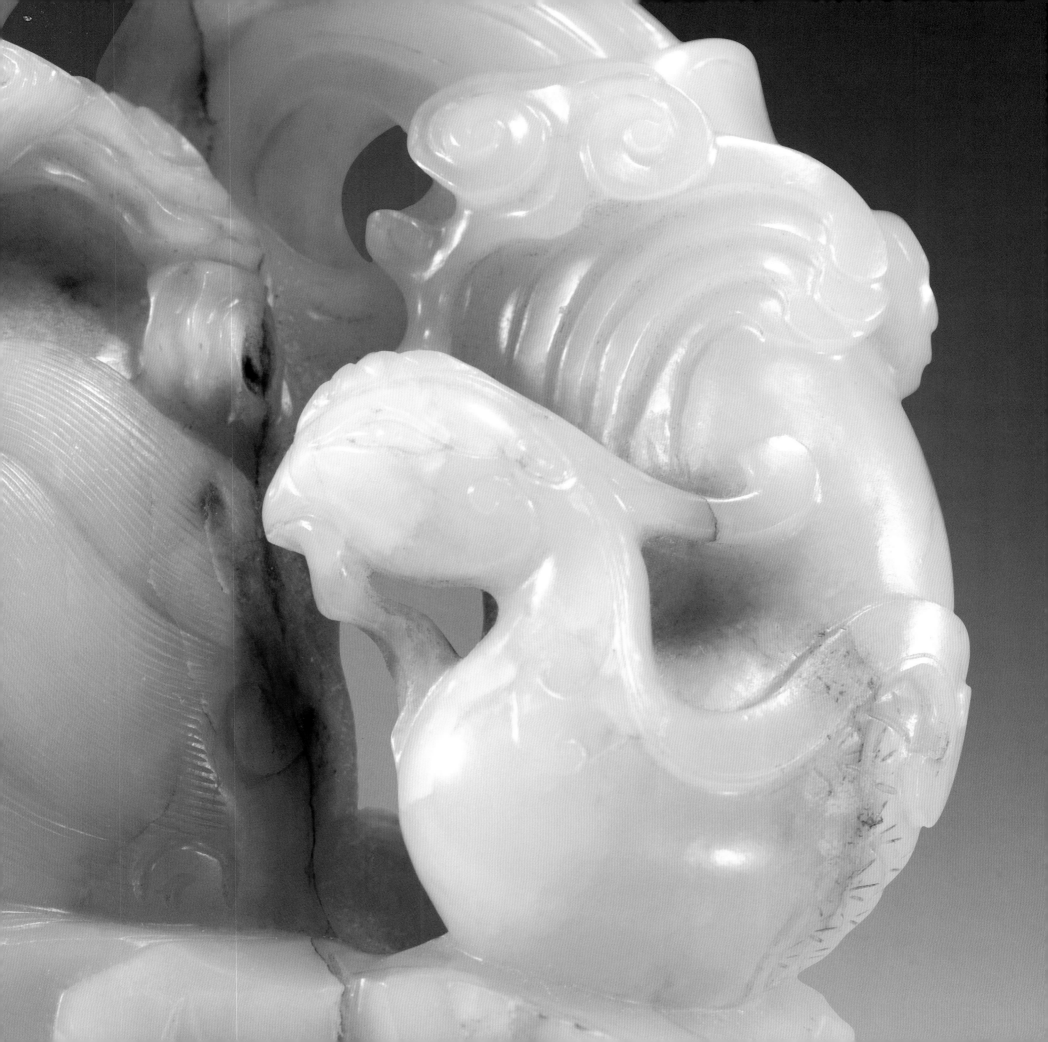

青白玉螭耳杯

明
高 7厘米   长 15.8厘米

　　青白玉质，玉质发灰，有皮色。整体造型为一椭圆形玉杯，直壁平底，壁较厚。杯身一侧镂雕一螭，另一侧则镂雕大小两只螭，成为玉杯的握柄。三螭皆曲颈弓身，口衔杯沿，四肢攀爬于杯壁之上，周围镂雕灵芝。玉杯双耳呈不对称式，抛光较好。

　　明代玉杯形制多样，纹饰丰富，螭耳杯为其中常见品种。

Greenish-white jade cup with *Chi*-dragon handles

Ming Dynasty (1368~1644)
Height 7cm   Width 15.8cm

　　The cup with an oval mouth is carved out of jade of gray hue. Parts of the cup retain the unpolished surface of the jade. Its bottom is flat and its walls are thick. On one side of the cup a *Chi*-dragon is sculpted and on the other side are two *Chi*-dragons, one large and the other small, shaped as the handles of the cup. The three *Chi*-dragons all bend their necks and bodies, with their lips holding the rim of the cup, and their legs on the wall of the cup. Around them, glossy ganoderma are carved. The two handles are not symmetrical.

　　Well polished, this cup with rich ornamentation is typical of Ming-dynasty cups with sculpted *Chi*-dragons.

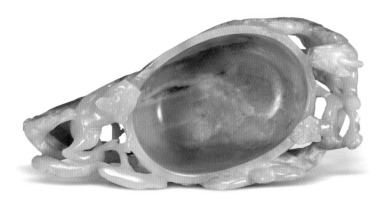

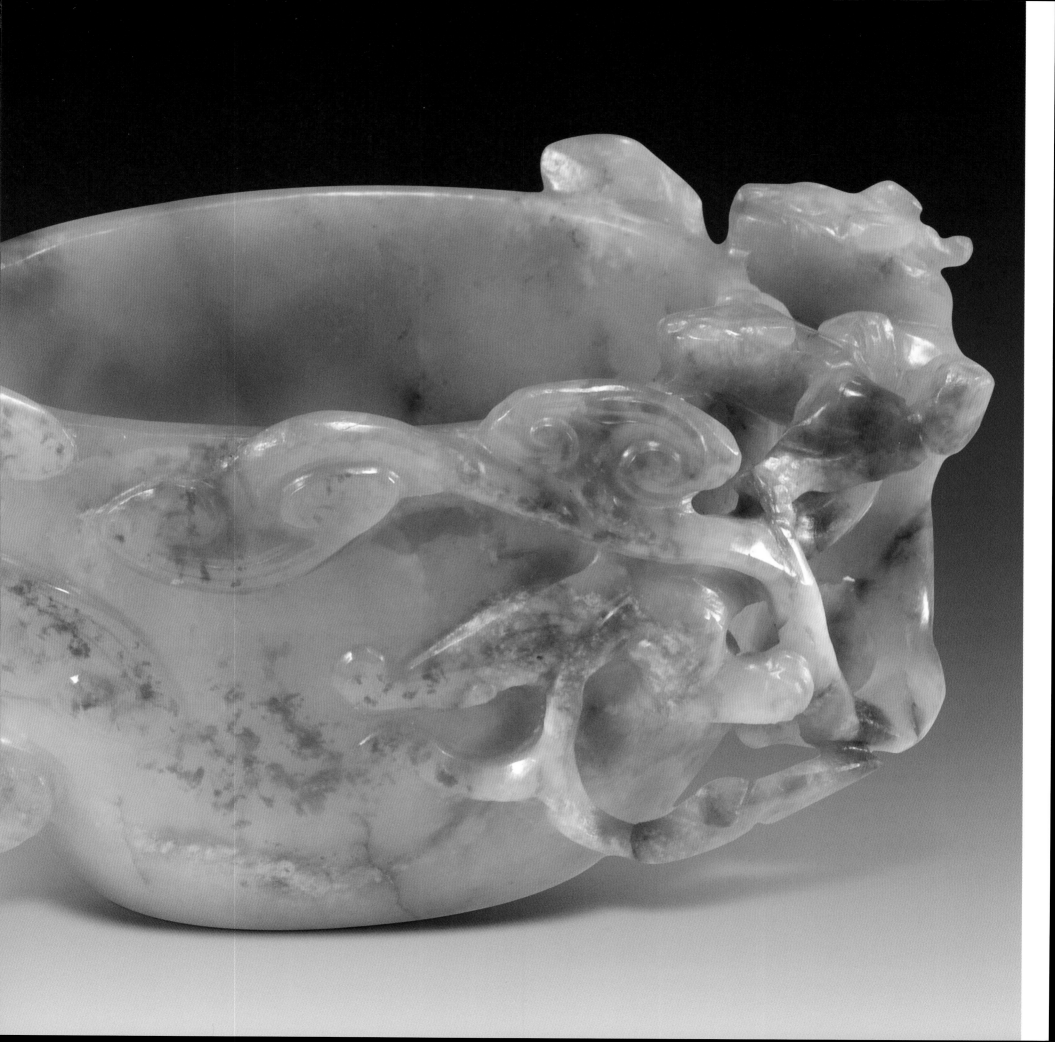

青玉双鱼纹荷叶式盘

明
长 17厘米　宽 13.7厘米

　　青玉质，多绺。以四边向内翻卷的荷叶为盘，整体呈圆角长方形。盘的内部中心凸饰两条头尾相接的游鱼，一鱼身饰鳞纹，另一鱼身饰米字纹，尾巴均张开似开放的花朵。双鱼周围用阴刻线琢出叶脉纹，与之相呼应的是盘的背面以隐起的阳线示叶脉，在细节处彰显其构思巧妙。

　　由于受到外来文化影响，同时也为了增强其实用性，在清末时期为此玉盘配以银托，银托以莲藕、荷花为题材。盘的窄边两端为银质荷叶及莲藕，盘底由二组银质荷花、荷叶和莲蓬构成底托，做工精细。银托与玉盘搭配可谓相得益彰。

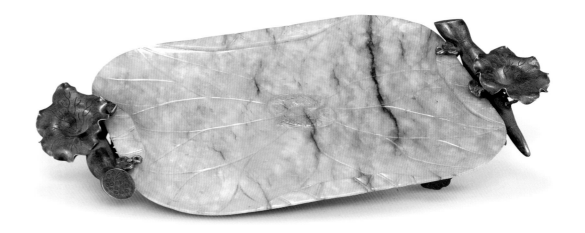

Green jade lotus leaf shaped plate with two fish design

Ming Dynasty (1368~1644)
Length 17cm　Width 13.7cm

　　Made of green jade with multiple veins, the round-cornered rectangular plate is formed by sculpturing lotus leaves turned inward from four sides. At the center of the plate are two parallel fish carved in relief, their heads pointing in opposite directions. One fish bears designs of scales, and the other is decorated with designs of the Chinese character for rice "*Mi*". The fish tails fan out in the shape of blooming flowers. Around the fish are incised veins of leaves, while on the reverse of the plate, the veins of the leaves are cut in relief.

　　Influenced by foreign art as well as practical necessity, in the late Qing Dynasty silver supports were added to hold the plate. The supports have designs of lotus roots and flowers. Both ends of the shorter edges of the plate have silver lotus leaves and lotus roots. The bottom of the plate is supported by two groups of silver lotus flowers, leaves and pods. Exquisitely made, the silver support and the jade plate complement each other's beauty.

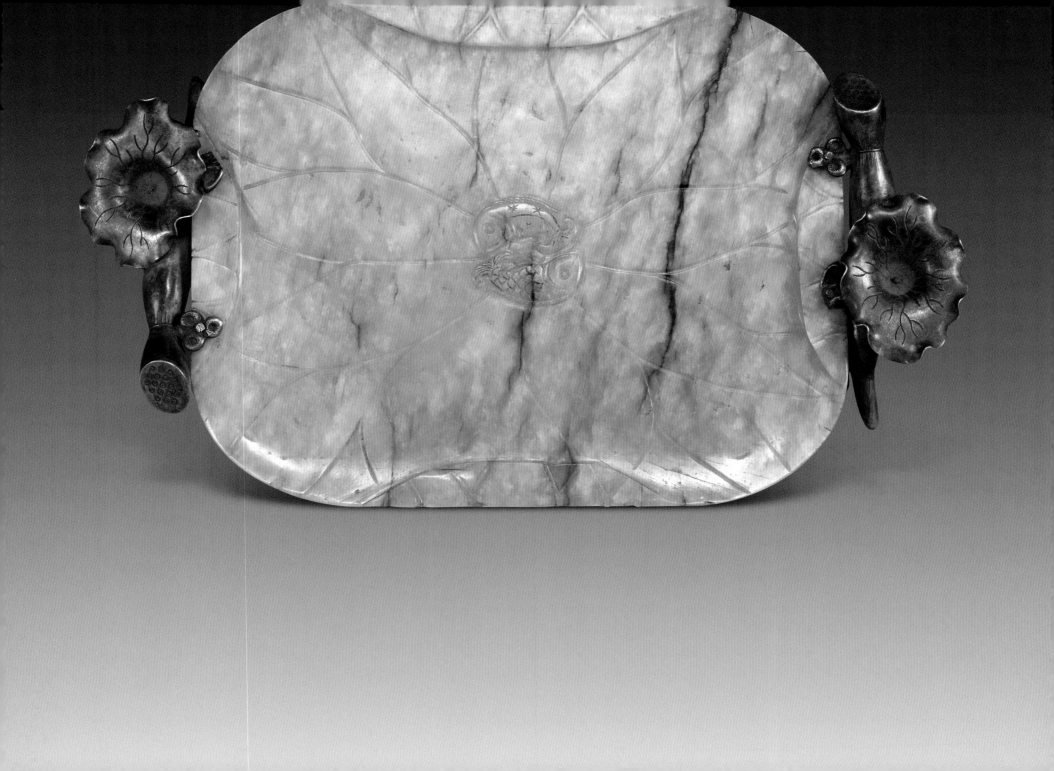

白玉夔龙纹佩

清乾隆
长 6.5厘米 宽 4.3厘米

　　白玉质，玉质温润致密。呈上窄下宽，上方中间有一圆形系孔。双面浮雕纹饰，各不相同。一面中间雕二个夔龙首，一向左一向右，龙上唇卷翘似回字形，下唇短，长耳长角。身体顺着玉佩环绕，体下有卷毛和足。身琢回形纹和云雷纹，以阴线刻划边线。另一面亦两龙，一龙首位于玉佩底端，目视系孔，圆眼，上吻卷，下吻短平。另一龙首平视，身躯环绕，上饰乳丁纹、卷云纹及云雷纹图案，边缘起棱或以阴线刻划。线条流畅自然，灵动矫健。这件玉佩将商周青铜器上的典型纹饰作为构图元素，古意盎然，体现了清乾隆朝仿古之风的盛行。

White jade pendant with *Kui*-dragon design

Qianlong Reign (1736~1795), Qing Dynasty
Length 6.5cm   Width 4.3cm

　　The material used is fine-grained, smooth white jade. The trapezium pendant has a hole for threading at the top, in the middle. On the front and rear of the pendant are reliefs of various designs. On one side, two heads of *Kui*-dragons are carved, one leftward and the other rightward. Their upper lips are curled and their lower lips are short. Their ears and horns are long. Their bodies wind round the pendant. Under their bodies are curls and feet. On their bodies are bas-reliefs of frets and clouds. There are two *Kui*-dragons on the other side too. One dragon's head is at the bottom of the pendant. The dragon looks at the hole with its round eyes. It upper lip is curled, and the lower lip is short and flat. The other dragon looks out at eye level and its body is winding, with designs of nail-heads and cirrus on it. The designs are outlined by sinuous, raised or engraved lines. The decoration of the pendant uses elements from Shang and Zhou-dynasties (c. 1600 BC ~ 476 BC) bronze objects, which exhibits the prevalent taste for ancient art during the reign of Qianlong (1736~1795).

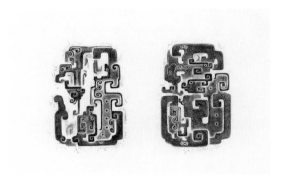

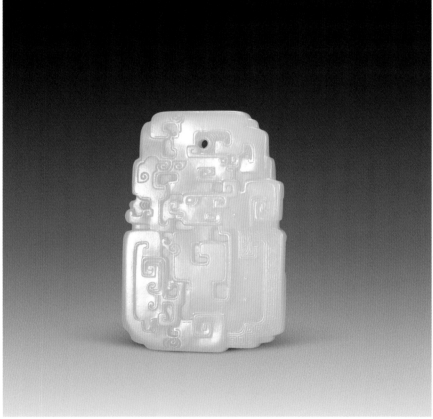

13

青白玉乾隆御题诗扳指

清乾隆
高 2.6厘米　径 3.1厘米

　　青白玉质，扳指呈直立的圆筒形，一端边缘内凹，由外侧向内侧微微向下倾斜，并有一圈黑色沁。另一端边缘则由外向内有少许凸出。外壁靠近上下边缘处各有一圈回纹装饰，中间以馆阁体楷书阴刻"乾隆御题"诗："缮人规制玉人为，彄沓闒抨是所资。不称每羞童子佩，如磨常忆武公诗。底须象骨徒传古，恰似琼琚匪报兹。于度机张慎省括，温其德美信堪师。"形制规整，碾磨精细。

　　扳指，古时是射箭时套在拇指上保护射手不被弓弦勒伤的环状器物，又称鞢，材质多样。随着时代的发展，其实用性越来越削弱，逐渐发展为象征身份地位的装饰品。清代乾隆皇帝对玉扳指极为钟爱，为诸多玉扳指写过不下50首诗作。当时宫廷御坊亦以御制诗为主要文字题材，因此在扳指上刻御制诗的作品较为多见。此件扳指与首都博物馆藏北京密云县董各庄清皇子墓出土的黄玉刻诗扳指和海淀博物馆藏北京皂君庙出土的白玉御题诗扳指形制、题材完全相同，是清代乾隆时期玉扳指的代表作品。

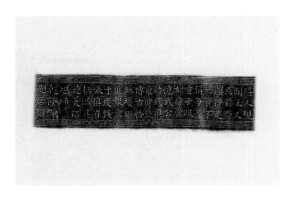

Greenish-white jade thumb ring with inscription of Emperor's poem

Qianlong Reign (1736~1795), Qing Dynasty
Height 2.6cm　Diameter 3.1cm

　　This thumb ring in the shape of an upright cylinder has one rim sloping down inward, with a ring of black trace of oozing. The rim on the other end slopes up inward. Near the top and bottom on the outer wall of the ring are bands of fret designs. At the middle section of the wall is an incised inscription of a poem by Emperor Qianlong, in regular script, reading: "The Marksman sets the specifications for the bows and arrows, the jade artisans produce the ring, to draw the bow and shoot the arrow. A bad archer may be ashamed that even a child could wear the ring. As Duke Wu's poem says, jade is polished fine and humans are cultivated to be noble. There is no need to use ivory to make a thumb ring as in ancient times. The material used is like a gem from the heavens. As one opens the bow, one must know moderation. The gentle quality of the ring is a virtue that man should learn from."

　　The thumb ring was worn over the thumb to protect archers' hands. It was made from different materials. With passage of time, its practical use diminished, and it gradually became an ornament. Emperor Qianlong was fond of jade thumb rings, and wrote no less than 50 poems about them. The Palace Workshop at that time had the emperor's poems engraved on its products; hence the abundance of imperial poems on thumb rings. The form of this thumb ring and the theme of the accompanying inscription are exactly the same as the topaz thumb ring with its incised inscription of a poem, unearthed from a Qing-dynasty prince's tomb in Dongge Village, Miyun County, Beijing, and the thumb ring in white jade unearthed from Zaojunmiao, Beijing, in the collection of the Haidian Museum. They are representative works of Qianlong's reign.

14

白玉三龙纹佩

清中期
长 7.1厘米　宽 4.2厘米

　　白玉质，玉质光洁盈润。佩琢三条龙，龙皆高额、大眼，长角，身躯呈"S"形或变形"S"形弯卷，三条龙的龙尾与龙身彼此相互缠绕纠结在一起，三龙身均圆润，光素无纹。此佩构思巧妙，碾磨精细，体现了高超的工艺水准。

White jade pendant with three dragons design

Mid-Qing Dynasty
Height 7.1cm　Width 4.2cm

　　This pendant from fine smooth jade was carved into the shape of three dragons, each with a protruding forehead, large eyes, long horns and a body bending in an S form. The tails and bodies of the three dragons are wound around each other. The bodies of the dragons are all plain. The ingeniously conceived and finely polished pendant displays superb workmanship.

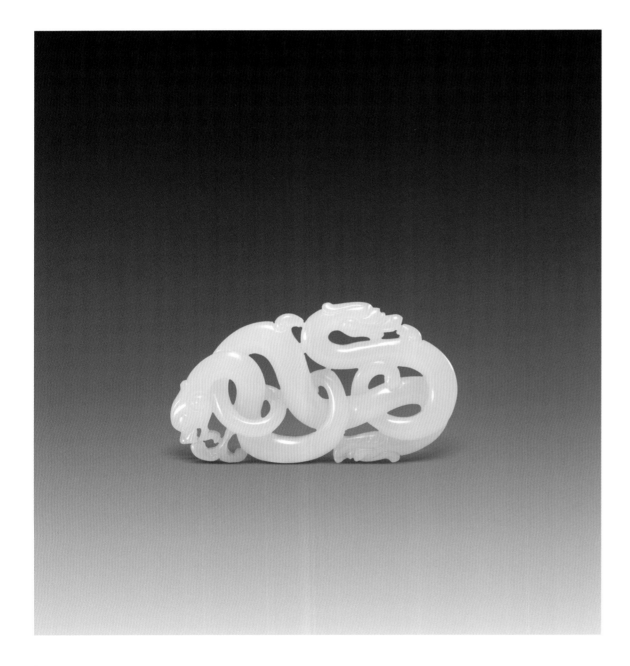

15

白玉夔凤纹佩

清中期
长 3.4厘米　宽 2.2厘米

白玉质，玉质莹润洁白。凤平视，额头高而饱满。凤尾呈"S"形向头上方弯折，尾尖下卷回收，形成佩的圆穿孔。身饰卷云纹。此佩线条流畅，碾琢精细，为典型的盛清之作。

White jade pendant with *Kui*-phoenix design

Mid-Qing Dynasty
Length 3.4cm　Width 2.2cm

The pendant in crystal clear jade is in the shape of a phoenix looking out at eye level. Its forehead is full and protruding, and its tail is raised in an S form, and the end of the tail is curled to form a hole for threading. On the bird's body are designs of clouds. The finely polished jade piece is a typical work of the high Qing Dynasty.

白玉螭龙纹四方佩

清中期
长 4.7厘米　宽 4.7厘米

　　白玉质，玉质温润细腻。琢四条螭龙缠绕交结，螭皆小耳张口，咬住前一条螭的腹部，身躯弯曲呈"几"字形，尾尖卷，抵另一螭的颈部，螭首向外，面朝四方。此佩构思精巧，取交结四方之意。

White jade pendant with design of four entwined *Chi*-dragons

Mid-Qing Dynasty
Length 4.7cm　Width 4.7cm

　　Carved from smooth and fine white jade, four *Chi*-Dragons are entwined around each other, and all having small ears, each holding another's belly with its mouth. All the dragons curl their backs up in the shape of inverse U, and each dragon touches another's neck with its tail. The dragons all point their heads outward in four directions. The Chinese for "entwined" is *Jiaojie*, a pun on "connection" or "making friends." The four directions stand for all the places in the world. So the whole piece is an allegory for "making friends all over the world."

白玉"增华进爵"铭牌

清中期
长 5.4厘米　宽 3.1厘米

　　白玉质，玉质温润莹泽。牌首为海水纹，中间一系孔，用于穿系佩戴。牌面呈"亚"字形。正面留边压地凸雕一枝梅花，其中一朵正在兀自开放，下琢青铜古爵一尊。背面中间琢长方形框，内琢阳文篆书"增华进爵"四字，其上饰阴刻花朵纹。牌底饰云纹。进爵乃加官之意，此牌两面图文互为呼应，形制规整，玉质上佳，雕琢精细。寓意步步高升，前程锦绣。

White jade plate with design of flowers and a *Jue* vessel

Mid-Qing Dynasty
Length 5.4cm　Width 3.1cm

　　The material used is smooth crystal jade. At the top of the oblong plate are designs of waves, and at the center is a hole for threading. On the front of the plate are boughs of plum blossoms, one of which is open. Below the flowers is an ancient vessel, *Jue*. On the rear is a rectangular border at the center, with an inscription in seal script in relief, reading, "Adding blossoms and presenting a *Jue*." A flower is incised above it. At the bottom of the plate are designs of clouds. These motifs are a pun on the Chinese phrase, "Promotion of rank and official position," since *Jue* is a kind of wine vessel while also meaning "rank." Meticulously carved and polished, the designs and inscription convey a hope of continual promotion in rank, and a bright future in officialdom.

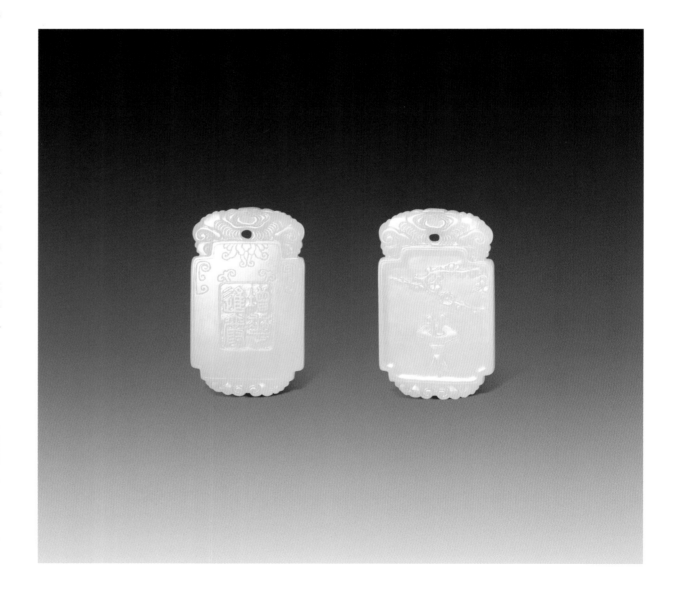

白玉御题诗文瓅子

清中期
高 3厘米　口径 1.6厘米

　　白玉质，玉质纯净温润。瓅子为圆柱状，上下有通天孔。器身上有阴刻楷体文字："璞非为贵追琢成器陈设满堂光辉献瑞砻錯之而拂拭 御题。"此器虽小，却尽显精巧雅致，颇具文人气息。

White jade *Lezi* tube with inscription of Emperor's poem

Mid-Qing Dynasty
Height 3cm　Diameter 1.6cm

　　The hollow tube has an incised inscription in regular script reading: "Crude jade is not valuable, but through polishing is made into an instrument. Many jade articles when displayed lend brilliance and an auspicious air to the hall. Jade is processed through filing, grounding and polishing. Inscription of the Emperor." Small as it is, the tube is an aesthetic object that caters to scholarly tastes.

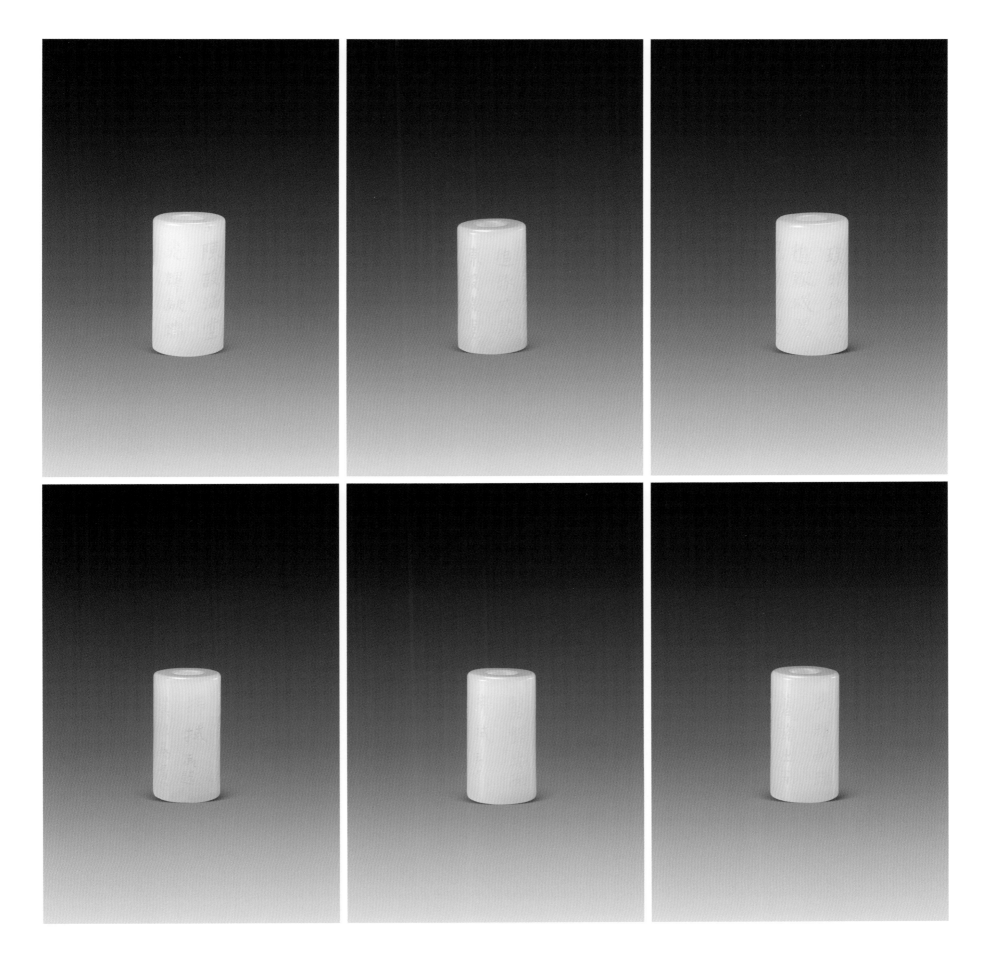

棚　　　龔　　　尖

找　　　鎗　　　耀

除　　　止　　　敲

眼　　　而　　　碧

莫非鳶書　狙承成器　陳設滿堂

白玉凤桃形坠

清中期
高 4.7厘米　长 5.7厘米

　　白玉质，玉色略闪青。为一块籽料随形雕琢而成，局部有皮色。正面整体为一凤鸟啄一寿桃造型，凤鸟回首立于寿桃之上，弯颈低头啄寿桃。凤鸟尖喙，圆眼，脑后和下巴各有一撮卷毛，身饰繁复的羽状纹，羽尖内卷。底部也琢有纹饰。此坠造型圆润，雕工洗练，碾磨精细，堪称清代中期玉雕佳作。

White jade pendant in the shape of phoenix and peach

Mid-Qing Dynasty
Height 4.7cm　Length 5.7cm

　　This ornamental artifact is carved from a nugget of grayish white jade which lends its overall shape to the sculpture, with a part showing the original color of its surface before polishing. At the front is a phoenix standing on a peach, turning its head to peck at the peach. The phoenix has a sharp beak and round eyes. On its body are meticulously carved feathers. The bottom of the sculpture is also ornamented with designs. The peach is a traditional symbol of longevity. The smoothly polished article is a fine piece dating back to the middle of the Qing Dynasty.

白玉击鼓童子形坠

清中期
高 3.1厘米　长 4.2厘米

　　白玉质，玉质光洁细腻。采用圆雕技法雕琢而成。童子作蹲跪状，左手扶鼓，右手执如意背于脑后，如意上挂一磬。童子笑容可掬，神态生动。

　　击鼓童子是明清时期较为常见的题材，寓意生活美满如意，太平盛世吉祥。此坠玉质上佳，造型精准，琢刻细腻，线条流畅，是清代中期玉雕童子题材中的典型作品。

White jade pendant in the shape of child beating a drum

Mid-Qing Dynasty
Height 3.1cm　Length 4.2cm

　　Meticulously carved from very smooth fine jade, this round sculpture presents a squatting child holding a drum in his left hand. In his right hand he holds an S-shaped ruler behind his head. The child with his broad smile appears lifelike.

　　A child beating a drum, a common theme from the 15th century to the 19th century, symbolizes a happy life and an orderly prosperous reign. Carved with flowing lines and finely polished, this realistic statuette is a typical work of a jade sculpture representing children, produced during the middle of the Qing Dynasty.

白玉花卉纹香囊

清中期
长 4.7厘米　宽 4.1厘米　通厚 1.1厘米

　　白玉质，玉质润白细腻。香囊整体似心形，由形状、纹饰完全相同的两部分组成，有子母口。采用镂雕技法雕琢花卉纹，雕工精致，线条流畅，打磨细致。

　　中国有着悠久的焚香历史，为达到行有香的效果，人们往往在腰间佩戴香囊，至清代佩戴香囊是相当普及的事情。宫廷的香囊，多用白玉制作，以昭显主人身份的显赫。此件香囊可以利用顶部和底部的镂孔，将前后两部分穿缀固定在一起，供系佩。

White jade fragrance bag with flower design

Mid-Qing Dynasty
Length 4.7cm　Width 4.1cm　Overall thickness 1.1cm

　　Made of fine, smooth white jade, the fragrance bag in the shape of a heart consists of two identical pieces of jade with identical patterns. The two pieces are combined by sinking the double rim of one piece into the double rim of the other. The patterns of flowers are cut in fluent line and finely polished.

　　Burning incense and using perfume for good scent is a lasting tradition in China. To have sweet scent while walking, Chinese people used to have a perfume pouch or case at their waist. Most perfume cases used in court are made of white jade, which marked the bearer's illustrious status. The two pieces of fragrance bag can be bound by stringing them through the holes on its top and bottom.

白玉素扳指

清中期
高 2.5厘米　径 3.1厘米

　　白玉质，玉质润若羊脂。扳指呈直立圆筒状，形制规整。一端由内侧边缘向外侧边缘微微向下倾斜，形成微凸的斜坡。另一端则反之，微微内凹。通体光素无纹，这样的处理往往对玉材的要求比较高。此扳指用料讲究，玉质洁白润泽，打磨精细，可谓完美的体现了材质之美。

White jade plain thumb ring

Mid-Qing Dynasty
Height 2.5cm　Diameter 3.1cm

　　The jade used for making this thumb ring is as smooth as suet. The ring is in the shape of an upright cylinder. At one end it has a rim sloping from the inner to the outer side, and on the other end, a reverse, slightly convened sloping is found. A plain thumb ring could only be made from very fine jade. This plain thumb ring reveals the quality of the material utilized.

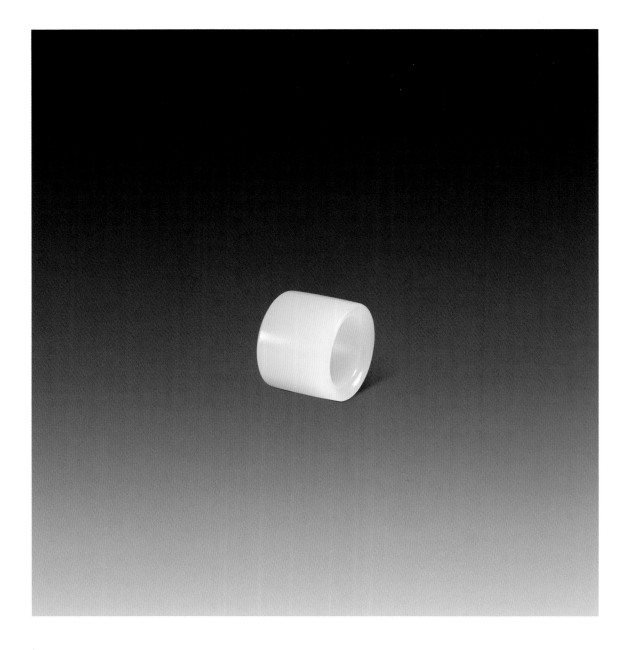

白玉云龙纹扳指

清中期
高 2.7厘米　径 2.9厘米

　　白玉质，玉质温润细腻。扳指呈直立圆筒状，一端口沿微凸，另一端呈坡状。外壁满饰云龙纹，线条婉转流畅，碾磨精细。

White jade thumb ring with design of cloud and dragon

Mid-Qing Dynasty
Height 2.7cm　Diameter 2.9cm

　　The thumb ring is in form of an upright cylinder with a slightly protruding rim at one end and a sloping rim on the other. On its wall are designs of dragons and clouds engraved in sinuous lines. It is finely polished.

白玉四喜纹扳指

清中期
高 2.6厘米　径 3.1厘米

　　白玉质，玉质细润。扳指呈直立圆筒状，外壁减地平雕四只喜鹊，或飞或立或驻于枝头或低头觅食。喜鹊圆眼，尖喙，长尾，双爪粗壮。此扳指布局疏朗，雕工精细。

White jade thumb ring with design of four magpies

Mid-Qing Dynasty
Height 2.6cm　Diameter 3.1cm

　　Carved from fine and smooth jade, the thumb ring is an upright cylinder. Its wall has four magpies sculpted by removing the surrounding surface of the jade. The magpies are flying, alighting on branches and pecking food on the ground. They have round eyes, long beaks, long tails, and strong thick claws. The image on the thumb ring is a well-balanced composition, and the whole piece is meticulously carved.

白玉狩猎纹扳指

清中期
高 2.3厘米　径 2.9厘米

　　白玉质，玉质洁白莹润，局部有黑沁。扳指呈直立圆筒状，以浮雕、镂雕技法雕琢而成。主题纹饰为狩猎图，中间浮雕一人着长袍戴官帽，低首垂目，骑马疾行，追逐前方的长角鹿，鹿作奋力奔跑状。周围浮雕出低矮的树枝和嶙峋的山石，并采用透雕技法雕出成组的四瓣花式纹。此扳指构图严谨，雕琢精细。

　　扳指时至清代，随着政权的巩固，征战的减少，逐渐成为一种象征身份的装饰品。骑射被认为是满族的立国之本，而在骑射必不可少的辅助性工具——扳指上琢刻狩猎纹，无疑是十分贴切其原本含义的，十分耐人寻味。

White jade thumb ring with hunting design

Mid-Qing Dynasty
Height 2.3cm　Diameter 2.9cm

　　Carved from crystal clear jade with a trace of black oozing, this thumb ring in the shape of an upright cylinder has reliefs and hollowed-out designs. The theme of the carving is the hunt. At the center of the scene is a man in a robe and official hat, lowering his head and spurring his horse on after a deer at the fore. The deer runs forward desperately. Around him are low trees and craggy hills. Beside are open carvings of four flowers. The picture on the thumb ring is a close-knit composition, meticulously carved and polished. The thumb ring was put on the thumb of the right hand when an archer drew the bow.

　　By the Qing Dynasty the regime was consolidated, and wars had decreased. Consequently, the thumb ring became an ornament symbolizing the wearer's status. Riding and shooting were the foundation of the Manchurian regime. The hunting scenes were carved on the thumb ring as an indispensable tool for an archer, underlining its function.

青白玉花卉纹包袱瓶

清中期
高 12厘米　宽 7.5厘米

　　青白玉质，器形近似扁体椭圆形。整体表现织物包裹一瓶，仅露出装饰了一圈阴刻回纹的瓶口。束带系于瓶颈部打结并飘然下垂，包袱皮在瓶颈处随着束带形成自然褶皱，线条自然流畅。身饰花卉纹，显得生机勃勃。

　　包袱瓶又叫布袋瓶，其器形一般是在瓶身上饰一凸雕的包袱巾或者束带。"包袱"有"包福"、"抱福"之意，带有浓厚的吉祥寓意。此件器物造型别致，雕工精细，是清代中期案头陈设品中的佳作。

Greenish-white jade sack-shaped vase with flower design

Mid-Qing Dynasty
Height 12cm　Width 7.5cm

　　This upright flat bottle is so carved that its major part looks as if it is wrapped with a piece of fabric, its rim with incised frets being exposed on the top. At the neck of the bottle a bow appears tied with its ends hanging down. The neck of the bottle shows the wrinkles of the sack, carved in flowing lines. On the body of the wrapped bottle are decorative flowers.

　　Such a bottle is also known as a "bottle in a sack." The Chinese word for "wrapper" is *Baofu*, which is partly homonymous with the Chinese phrase "possessing fortune," hence an auspicious object. The meticulously carved bottle is a fine piece produced during the middle of the Qing Dynasty.

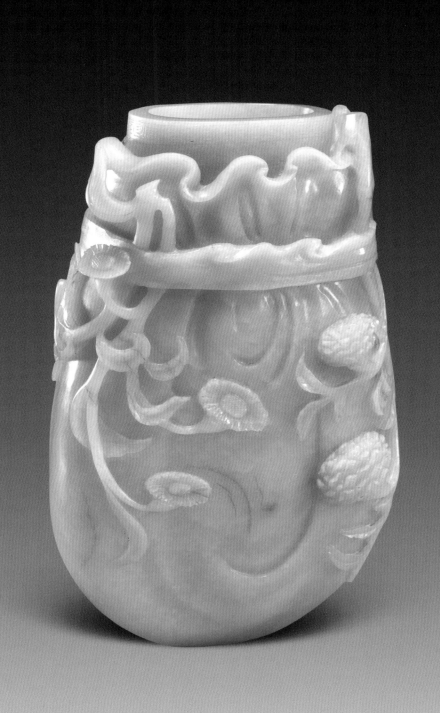

27

青白玉罗汉赞山子

清中期
高 19厘米　宽 20厘米

　　青白玉质，以整块籽玉随形雕琢而成。山子正面琢山崖状，崖洞中达摩长发卷须身披长袍微侧身体跪坐于台阶之上，右手执念珠，神态平和。崖洞右侧琢洞石及灵芝。山子背面雕琢两株松树傲然挺立于山石岩隙间。达摩上方垂下的山石上阴刻楷体诗文"罗汉赞　翠岩袖手，瓶钵不持，神通变化，无所之施。开眼见明，闭眼见暗，何处征心，本来弗欠。了心如幻，见身无实，画师写照，不殊面壁。"此玉山子整体构图疏密有致，浑厚大气，线条简洁硬朗，如刀砍斧凿一般，这与扬州山子"保形掏洞"的特点不同，应属于北京地区较为粗犷的"砍山子"风格。

Greenish-white jade mountain with inscription of *Ode of Arhat*

Mid-Qing Dynasty
Height 19cm　Width 20cm

　　The sculpture is carved from a whole jade nugget that lends its shape to the contours of the mountain. At the foot of the mountain is a cave. In the cave the peaceful Indian monk Bodhidharma (d. AD 536), with curly hair, sits in a three-quarter profile on a stone platform, his right hand holding a rosary. To the right of the cave are rocks, and glossy ganoderma – a herb seen as magical. Behind the mountain stand two pines. The inscription incised on the rock above Bodhidharma reads, "On the Arhat: Against green rocks, he has his hands in his sleeves, not bothering to hold a bowl for alms; his immense magical power has no place to be used. When his eyes open, light is seen. When his eyes are shut, darkness reigns. What one should think of is nothing at all. The mind is unreal, so the body is no solid matter. The artist precisely represents the enlightened master true to life." The mountain is carved with bold traces of cutting. Unlike mini-sculptures of mountains produced in Yangzhou with holes cut in them, this one is in the style of a Beijing creation, the surface of which is roughly polished.

羅

翠巖褴手鑷不

持神通變化無所

之施開眼見明心閉

眼見暗何處徵心如

本來弗欠了心如

幻見身無實畫師

寫照不殊面壁

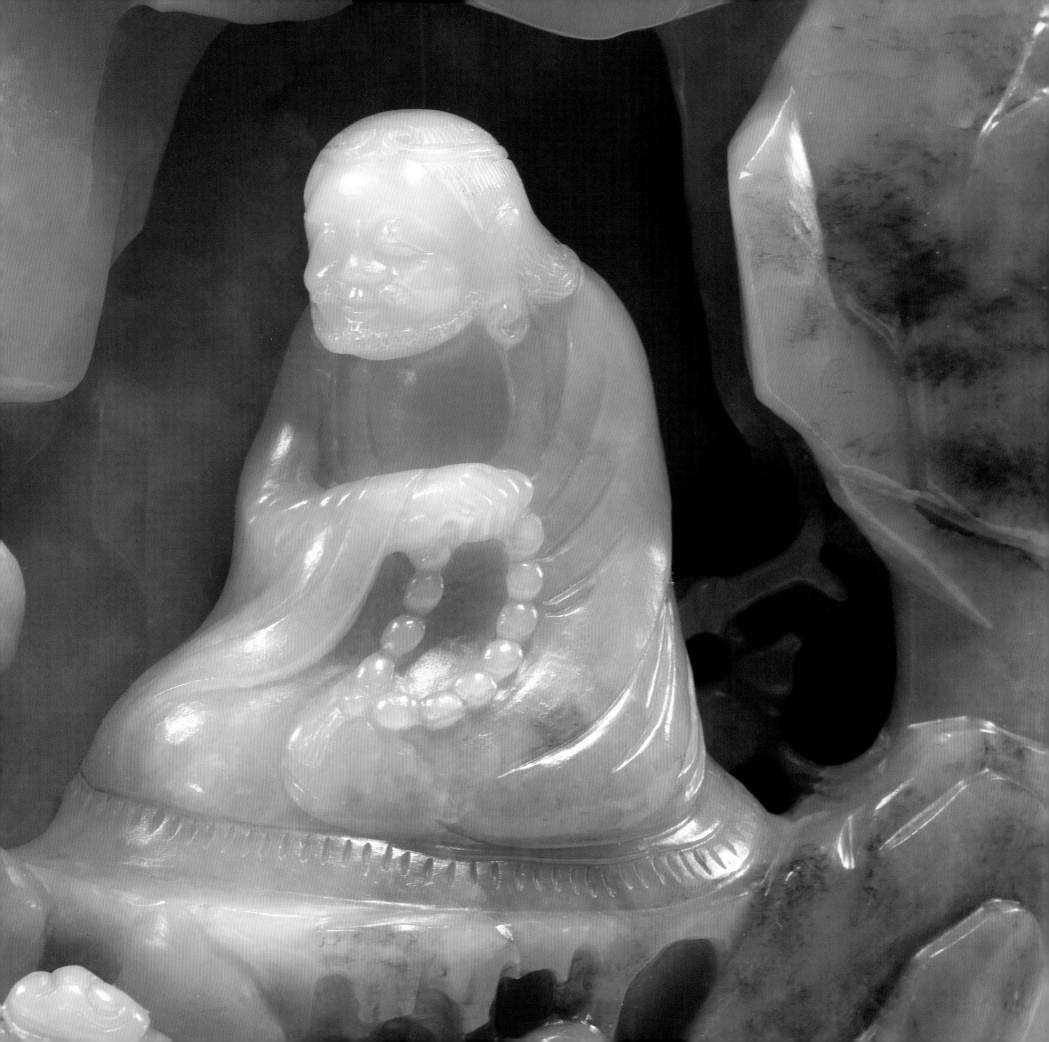

28

白玉龙纹环（一对）

清
直径 2.1厘米　厚 0.6厘米

　　白玉质，玉质洁白温润。一对，大小相同，纹饰相对。均采用浅浮雕和阴线刻划相结合的技法，正面琢一大一小二只螭龙，四目相对，此应为子母螭的形象。大螭脑后飘着长长的毛发。二螭身躯皆随环的弧度弯曲，雕出爪尾，并延伸至环的背面。此玉环材质精良，打磨细致，器形小巧，更显工艺精湛。

White jade ring with dragon design(A pair)

Qing Dynasty (1644~1911)
Diameter 2.1cm　Thickness 0.6cm

　　Carved in crystal clear white jade, this pair of rings is of identical diameter, and the designs on them are symmetrical. Both rings are decorated with reliefs and engravings. On the front of each are a large hornless dragon and a smaller one, looking at each other. They are mother and son. On the back of the large dragon's head are long drooping hairs. The bodies of the dragons bend along with the arc of the rings, their claws and tails extending to the back side of the rings. They are finely polished.

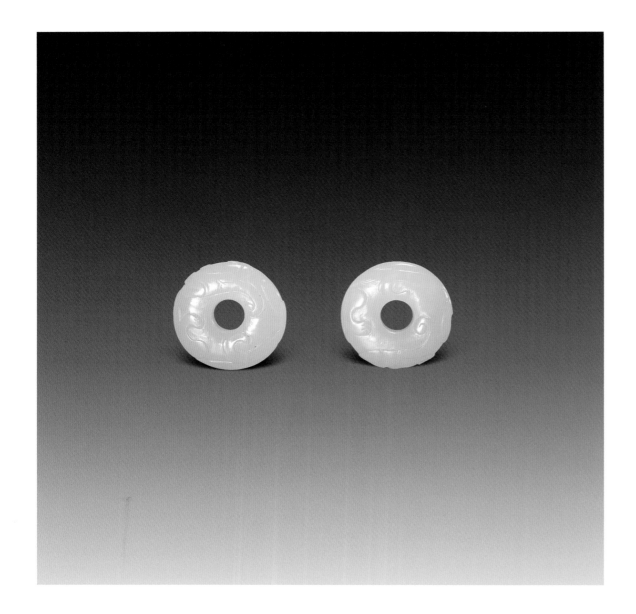

29

白玉子辰佩

清
长 11.3厘米　宽 5.8厘米

　　白玉质，扁圆环形。宽缘，边缘光滑，双面浅浮雕，正面为篆体"子、丑、寅、卯、辰、巳、午、未、申、酉、戌、亥"十二地支，背面为八卦纹。环心镂雕一童子，头歪向一边，笑脸盈盈，双手及左腿抬起，呈舞蹈状。于环的窄缘两侧各立一螭龙，上下呼应，均回首，细眼长颈，尾垂于环的背面。子辰佩，多有望子成龙之意。此佩构思巧妙，料佳工精，寓意吉祥。

White jade pendant with design of child and dragon

Qing Dynasty (1644~1911)
Length 11.3cm　Width 5.8cm

　　This flat circular pendant has broad and smooth edges. Both sides bear bas-reliefs. On its obverse are characters in seal script for the 12 "earthly branches," namely, the 12 animals making up a cycle of years, each marking when a person is born; and on its reverse are augury trigram signs. At the center of the ring is an open carved child tilting his head and smiling. He raises his two hands and left leg to dance. On top of the pendant stands a dragon, and at its base another dragon. The two dragons turn their heads to look at each other. Both dragons have narrow eyes and long necks. Their tails curl behind the pendant. Ingeniously conceived and meticulously carved in fine material, this pendant delivers the message that the child will become a dragon – a "dragon" signifying a very successful person.

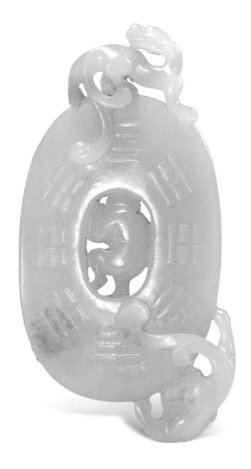

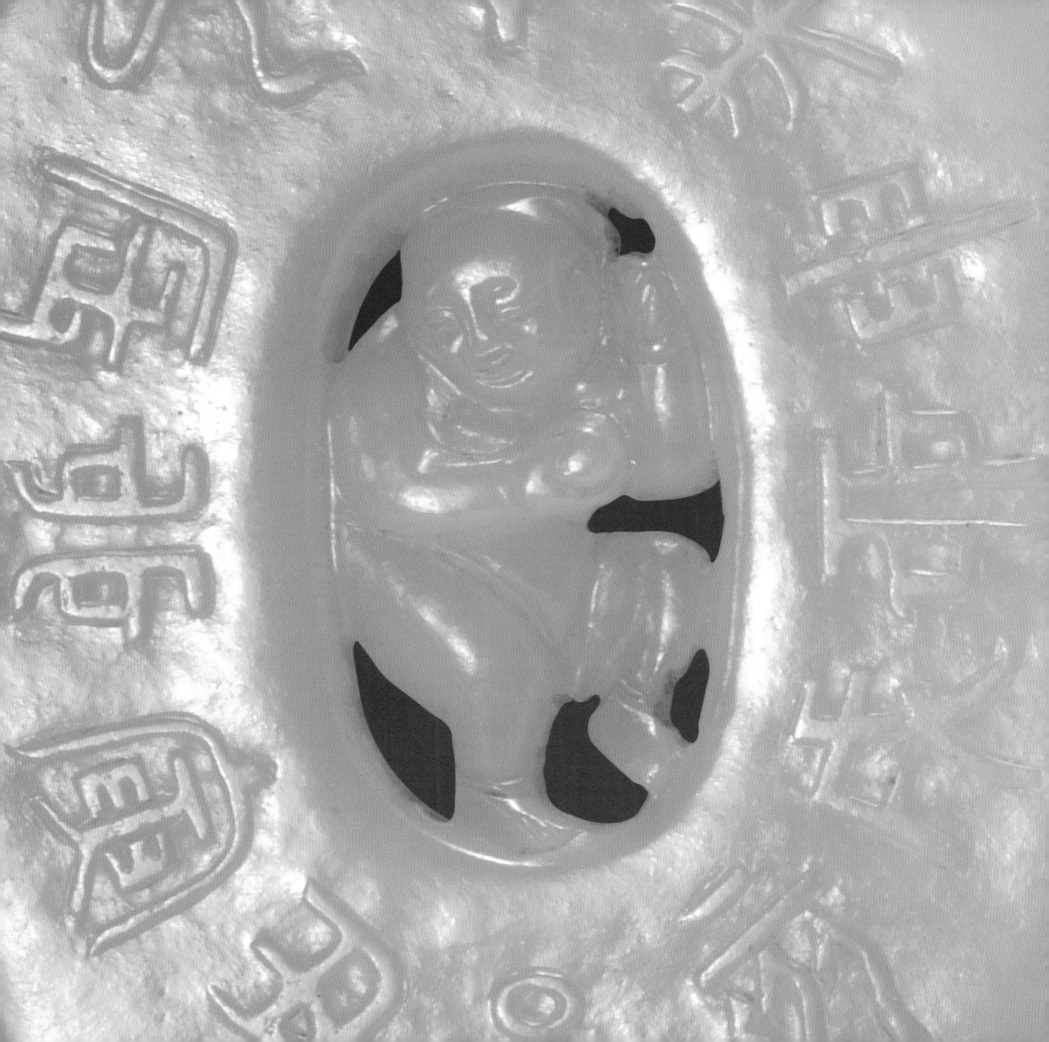

30

白玉刘海戏金蟾形坠

清
高 5.7厘米　宽 3.4厘米

　　白玉质，玉质莹润致密。刘海圆脸宽额，发中分，头略低，眼望下方，嘴角上翘，面露微笑。左手握一方孔圆钱置于胸前，右臂上曲手执扫帚背于脑后。上身着右衽衫，系腰带，下身着裤。右腿曲膝，足踩一金蟾，蟾鼓眼阔嘴，目视前方。此器雕工精细，人物刻画自然生动。

　　刘海戏金蟾是明清之际非常盛行的玉雕题材，寓意驱邪佑福、百利生财。

White jade pendant in the shape of Liu Hai playing with golden toad

Qing Dynasty (1644~1911)
Height 5.7cm　Width 3.4cm

　　Liu Hai is a legendary figure. In this statuette, Liu Hai has a round face with a broad forehead. His hair is parted at the centre. He lowers his head to look down; the corners of his mouth are raised to show a smile. He holds a Chinese coin (which has a square hole at its centre) in his left hand and a broom behind his head with his right arm. His garment is buttoned at the right. With a belt at his waist, he wears trousers. His left leg is bent to keep a toad under his foot. The toad has bulging eyes and a wide mouth, looking ahead. The sculpture is exquisitely carved to present the figure vividly.

　　Liu Hai playing with a golden toad was a popular theme for jade sculpture from the 15th to the 19th centuries. It is used to ward off evils and ensure acquisition of wealth.

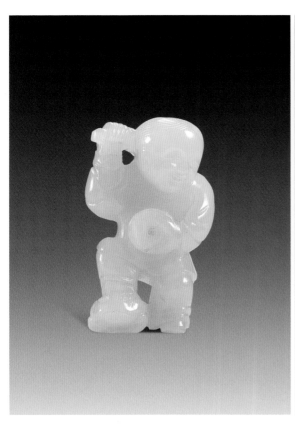

31

糖玉牛生麒麟形坠

清
长 4.3厘米　宽 3.3厘米

　　糖白玉质。巧妙利用玉料天然的糖白双色雕琢，糖玉圆雕成卧牛，牛角卷曲后展，脊背高耸，牛角与牛尾皆有阴刻线装饰。白玉部分则圆雕一麒麟，体积较牛纤巧，头上扬，口衔祥云洛书，身饰鳞纹。整体造型呈牛环抱麒麟状，牛与麒麟之间有一祥云状装饰。

　　牛与麒麟相结合的造型来源于"牛生麒麟，猪生象"的民间传说。明·沈德符《万历野获编·卷二九·禨祥》也有相关记载："麒麟之生，多托牛腹。"麒麟自古以来便被视为仁兽、瑞兽，牛生麒麟则预示着天降祥瑞，天下大吉。

Fawn jade pendant in the shape of a cow giving birth to a *Qilin*

Qing Dynasty (1644~1911)
Length 4.3cm　Width 3.3cm

　　The pendant is carved using the two natural colors of the jade. The fawn part was sculpted into a cow lying down with its horns going backward, and its back raised. The horn and tail of the cow have incised ornamentation. The white segment is sculpted into a *Qilin* whose body is more slender than the cow. The *Qilin*, with its head raised, holds a book shrouded by auspicious clouds between its lips. Its body has designs of scales.

　　The cow holds the *Qilin*, and the clouds are carved between the two creatures. The images in this pendant derive from an old popular belief that cows give birth to *Qilin* and pigs give birth to elephants. This belief is also found in "Auspicious Signs" in Vol. 29 of Shen Defu's (1578~1642) Hearsay of the Wanli Reign (Wan Li Ye Huo Bian): "The *Qilin* are born from cows' abdomens." The *Qilin* has been regarded as a kind and auspicious animal from ancient times. A cow giving birth to a *Qilin* augurs good tidings.

32

白玉龙纹手镯

清
直径 7.9厘米　宽 0.9厘米

　　白玉质，玉质细腻洁白。整体造型为一龙，口衔龙尾，形成近似圆形的圈口。龙身细长，呈扭曲状。龙高额凸目，长吻齐平，张口衔龙尾。尾尖卷曲。颈部饰波纹及阴刻长发，尾部饰鳞纹。龙睛用细小的珍珠镶嵌，额头正中嵌有一粒剖面为圆形的红珊瑚，珊瑚色彩艳丽，与白玉搭配相得益彰。

　　玉镯的起源很早，在新石器时代即已出现，明清时期是玉镯使用的高峰时期，较为常见，但采用如此精致的工艺装饰的白玉龙纹镯实属罕见。

White jade bracelet with dragon design

Qing Dynasty (1644~1911)
Diameter 7.9cm　Width 0.9cm

　　Made of fine white jade, the bracelet is shaped as a dragon's mouth holding its tail. The twisting body of the dragon is slim and long. Its forehead bulges and eyes protrude. The long snout has a flush end. On its neck are wave designs and incised long hairs; on its tail are designs of scales. Tiny pearls are embedded in its eyes, and a brilliant red coral bead is embedded at the center of its forehead.

　　The jade bracelet dates back to the Neolithic Age. The Ming and Qing dynasties saw a booming production of jade bracelets, but few are as beautifully and meticulously ornamented as this one.

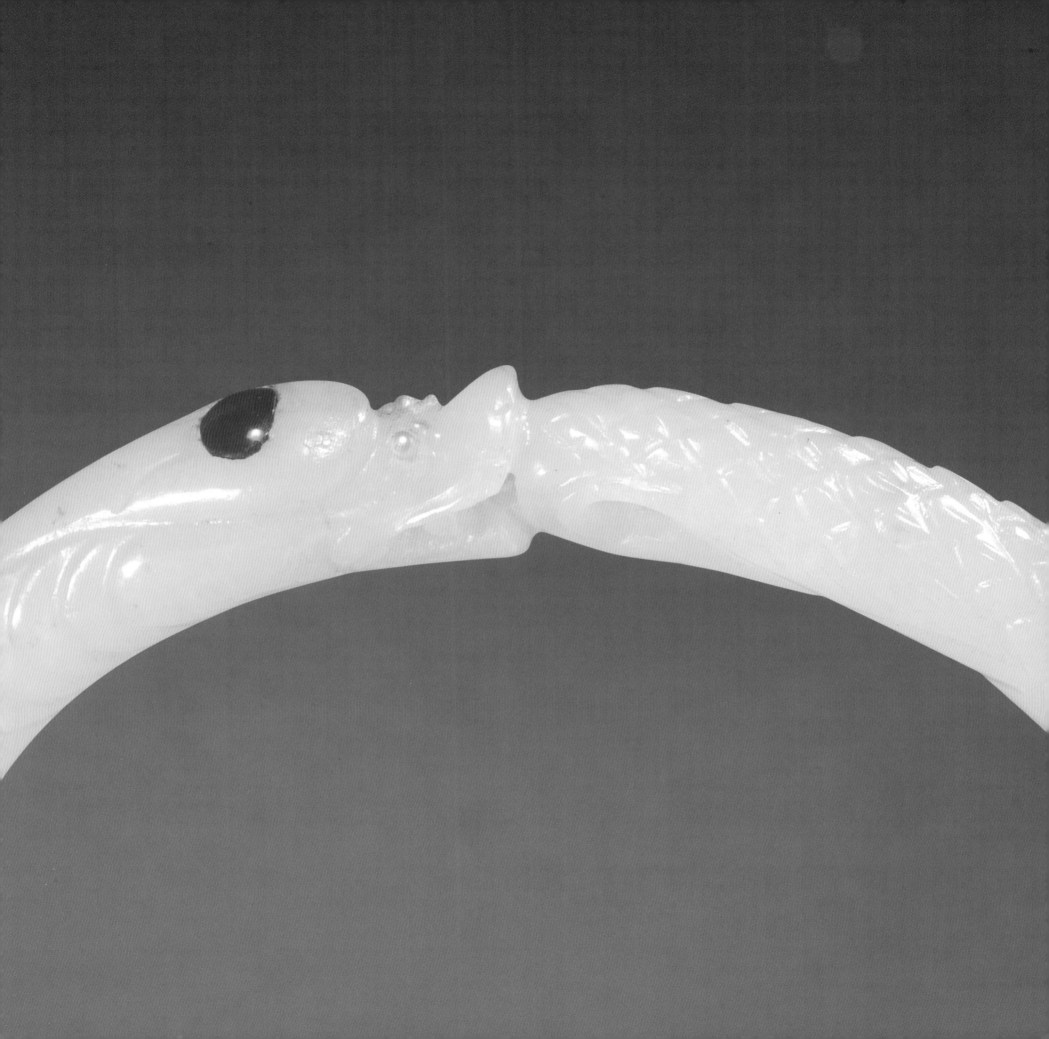

33

白玉龙首螭纹带钩

清

长 10.3厘米　宽 2.9厘米

　　白玉质。钩首为龙首，双角，小耳，杏眼，弯眉，嘴拱平齐。钩身上浮雕一螭，呈曲身向前状，与龙首四目相对。钩背面雕一扁圆形钮，钮为花形，上以阴刻线示蕊。

　　元明清时期制作的玉带钩数量不仅多，其形制也多样，已由实用器物逐渐转变成玩赏型器物。此时期玉带钩的形制以龙首形最多，尤以龙螭纹相组合的带钩最为常见。因螭是龙的九子之一，故这种龙螭组合的带钩有"苍龙教子"的含义。

White jade belt buckle with *Chi*-dragon design

Qing Dynasty (1644~1911)
Length 10.3cm　Width 2.9cm

　　One end of the buckle is in the shape of a dragon's head with two horns, small ears, round eyes, curved eyebrows and a flush snout. On the buckle is the relief of a *Chi*-dragon, whose body is bent in an S-form, looking into the eyes of the dragon at the end of the buckle. The back of the buckle is carved into an oval button in the shape of a flower, the stamen of which is presented by incision.

　　From the Yuan through the Qing dynasties (1279~1911), a large number of belt buckles in various forms were produced. Gradually, the belt buckle turned from an object in daily use into one with aesthetic appeal. Most belt buckles during that period of time were decorated with designs of dragon heads, and most commonly a horned dragon with a hornless one. It was believed that one of the dragon's nine sons is hornless. So this design carried a message of a dragon instructing his sons.

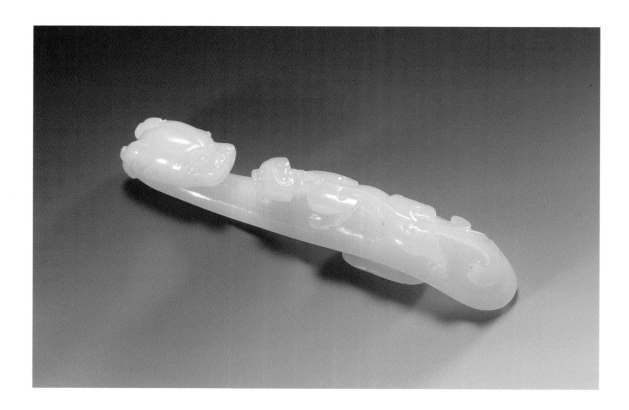

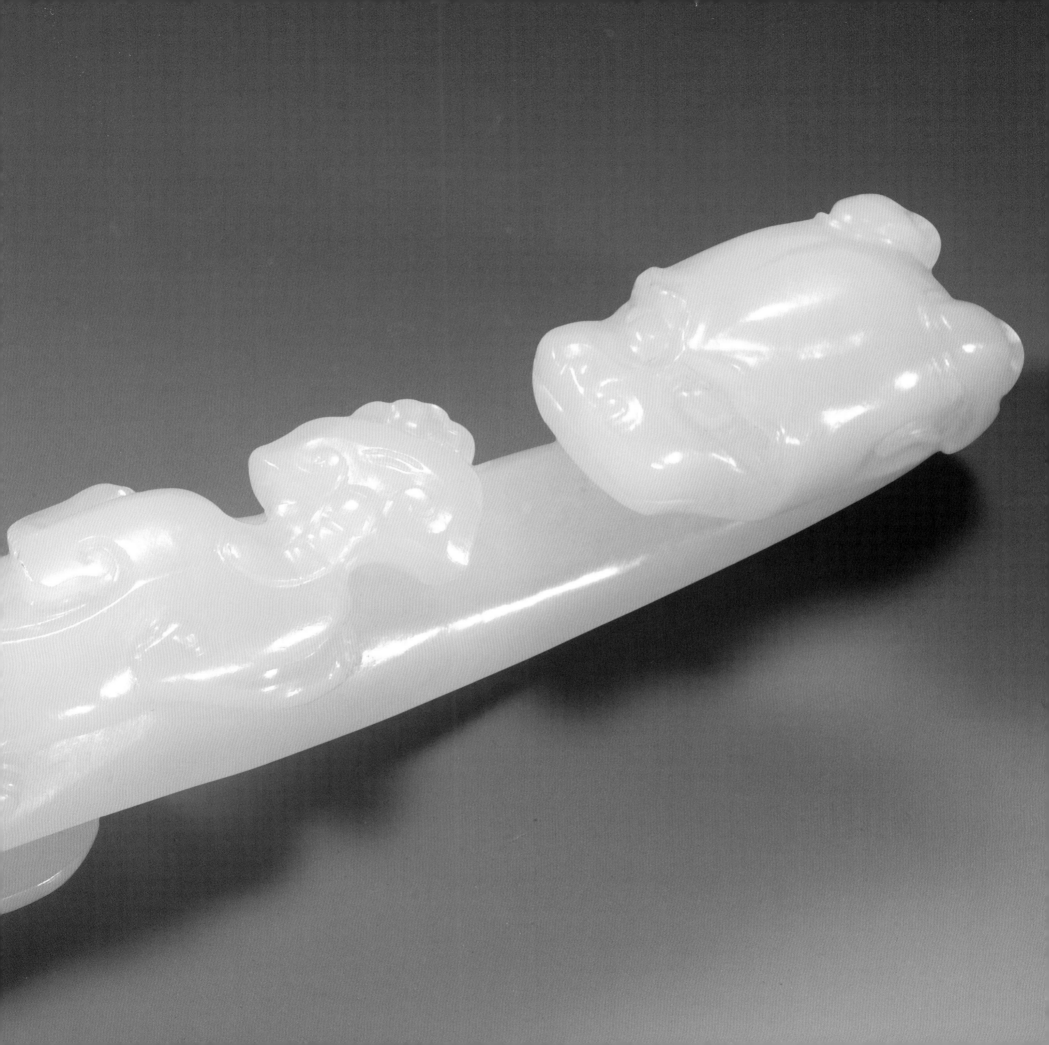

34

白玉龙首蝉纹带钩

清
长 8.6厘米　宽 2.9厘米

　　白玉质，玉质光洁莹润。钩首为龙首，大嘴宽平，张口露齿，眉毛向上弯卷，小尖耳，双角并齐，短而圆滑。钩身上浮雕蝉纹，蝉突眼，颈短而宽、颈部饰几道平行的波纹，翅膀呈八字形长而窄，尾作弧形收敛，背脊线隆起，双翼上饰云头纹等纹饰。钩背面雕一圆形钮。此带钩雕工流畅，琢磨精细，以蝉纹饰钩身的玉带钩较为独特，为清代中期带钩中的精品。

White jade belt buckle with dragon and cicada design

Qing Dynasty (1644~1911)
Length 8.6cm　Width 2.9cm

　　The buckle is made of smooth and bright jade. One end of the buckle is carved into the shape of a dragon's head, with a wide mouth, exposed teeth, upwardly curved eyebrows, and small sharp ears, including two short and smooth horns of equal length. On the buckle is a relief of a cicada with protruding eyes, a short and broad neck bearing several parallel lines as decoration, and long narrow wings. Its tail is drawn in a curve, its spine is a high ridge, and its wings bear designs of clouds. The back of the buckle has a carved round button. Belt buckles with designs of cicada are very hard to come across. This buckle, carved with exquisite craftsmanship and finely polished, is a masterpiece produced during the middle of the Qing Dynasty.

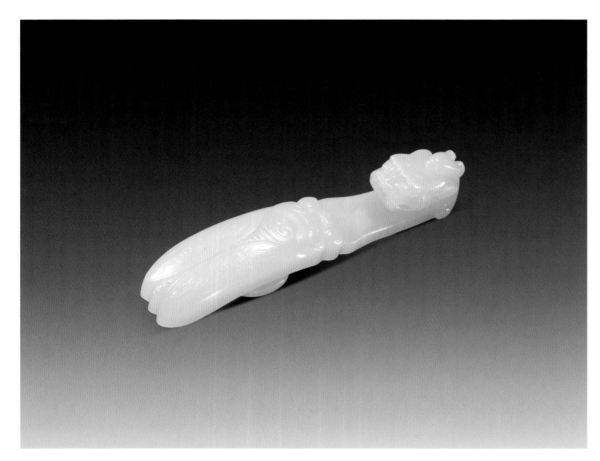

白玉螳螂捕蝉纹带钩

清
长 8.9厘米　宽 1.4厘米

　　白玉质，钩首琢为螳螂首造型，双眼圆而突出，向前注视，额头、鼻子均以云头形为饰。钩身上浮雕一只蝉，身躯细长，凸目，长鼻，双翅收拢，伏于钩尾。带钩背面一扁圆形钮。此件带钩玉质润白，刀法娴熟明快，题材暗合螳螂捕蝉之意。

White jade belt buckle with design of a mantis catching a cicada

Qing Dynasty (1644~1911)
Length 8.9cm　Width 1.4cm

　　One end of the hook is carved into a mantis with two bulging eyes gazing ahead and a snout in the shape of a cloud. On the buckle is a relief of a slim cicada with bulging eyes, a long nose, and wings drawn in. The back of the buckle has an oval button. The buckle which has the meaning of "a mantis catching a cicada" in Chinese culture is succinctly carved from a piece of smooth white jade.

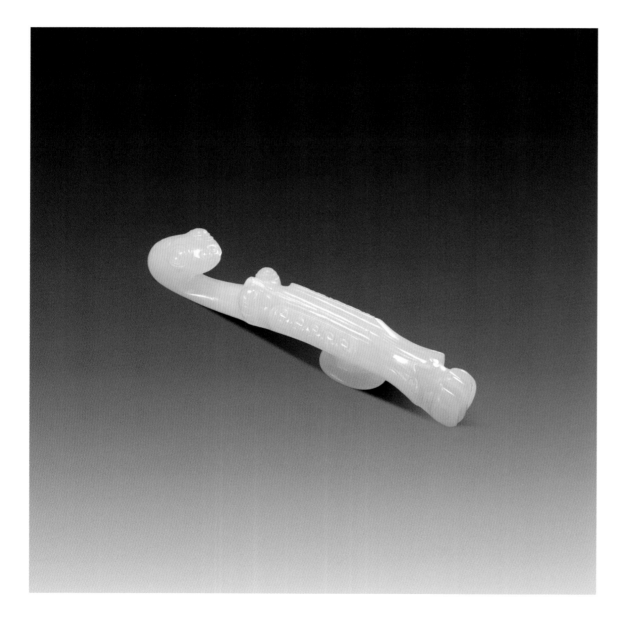

白玉瓶形带饰

清
长 5.5厘米　宽 3.9厘米

　　白玉质，玉质洁白润泽。正面为双耳瓶形，瓶侈口，丰肩，镂雕双耳，下腹斜收，底部呈一扁环，背面有长方形带扣。颈肩部位雕蕉叶纹，其下为水波纹。足部饰云头纹。此带饰可供穿在腰带上系物。

White jade amphora-shaped belt ornament

Qing Dynasty (1644~1911)
Length 5.5cm　Width 3.9cm

　　The front of the ornament is a wide-mouthed amphora with pierced handles and large shoulders. Its lower half tapers off to the bottom. Banana leaves are engraved on its neck, with wave designs beneath them. Clouds designs are found on the bottom, and below that, a flat ring. The ornament can be threaded on a belt.

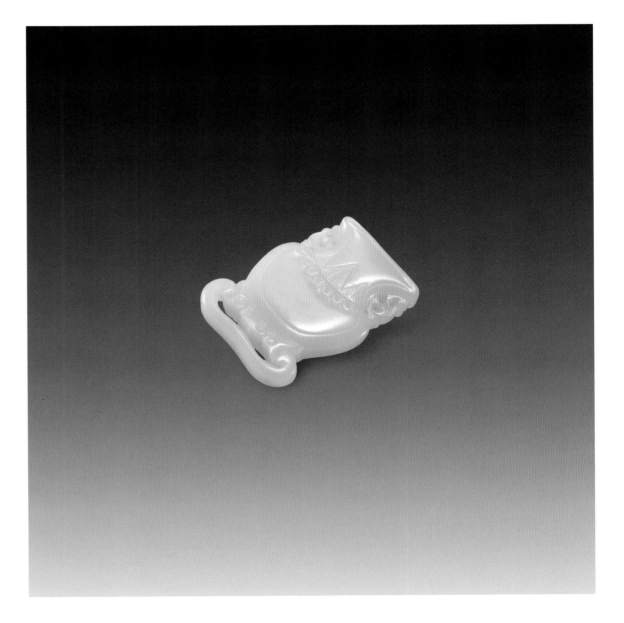

白玉五福捧寿纹饰件

清
直径 8.2厘米　厚 0.3厘米

　　白玉质，玉质细腻润泽。饰件呈圆形，留有窄边框，内雕琢等距分布的五只蝙蝠，蝙蝠展翅作飞行状，寓意五福捧寿，洪福齐天。地纹采用镂雕技法雕琢繁缛的缠枝莲纹及忍冬纹，最中间透雕一花朵。雕工精湛，堪称上品。

White jade ornament with five bats design

Qing Dynasty (1644~1911)
Diameter 8.2cm　Thickness 0.3cm

　　The circular piece has a narrow rim, and the five bats carved within the rim all spread their wings at regular intervals. The Chinese for "bat" is homonymous with the word for "fortune." The ground is pierced into designs of winding lotus and honeysuckle, with a flower at the center. The jade used is fine and smooth, and the carving is consummate.

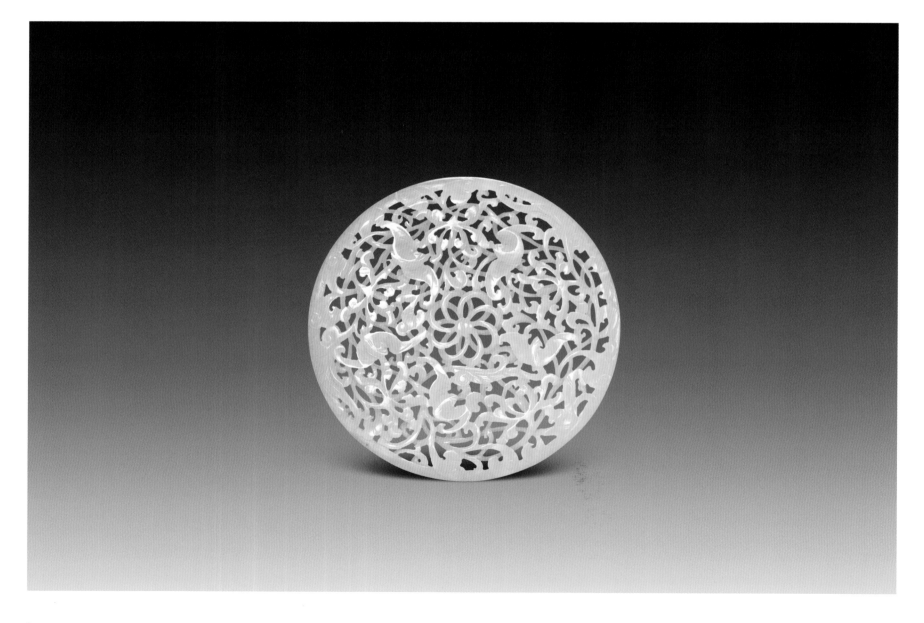

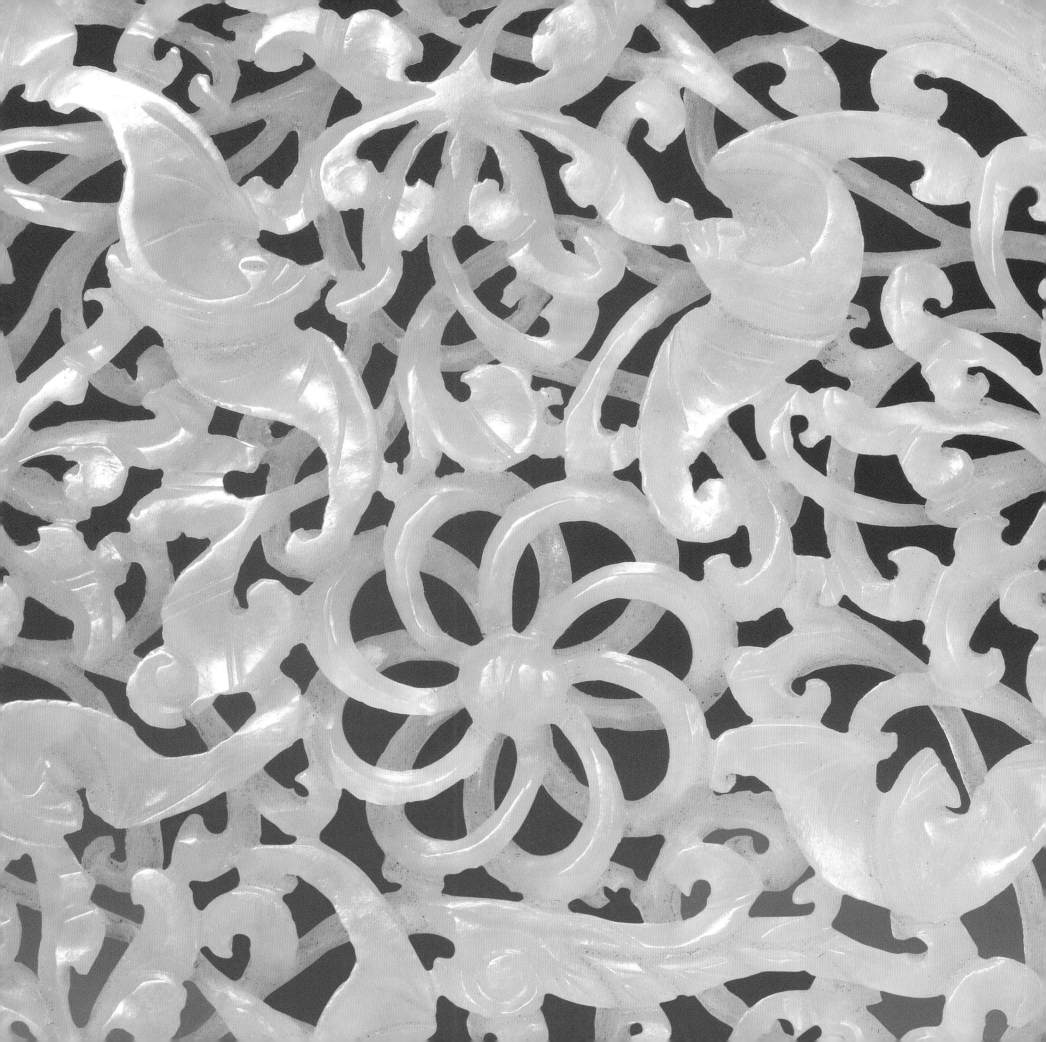

38

白玉福寿印章

清
高 3.5厘米　长 2.8厘米

　　白玉质，质洁无瑕。印身上浮雕蝙蝠和波涛
纹。印钮为兽形钮，兽独角，侧立，头扭向正面，
似在低头注视着蝙蝠，尾上翻搭于背臀部。"蝠
兽"谐音"福寿"，寓意吉祥。

White jade seal with bat design and knob in the shape of animal

Qing Dynasty (1644~1911)
Height 3.5cm　Length 2.8cm

　　The seal has reliefs of bats and waves on its sides.
Its knob is in the form of a animal with hooves turned
sideways, lowering its head to watch the bats. Its tail is
raised on its haunches. The Chinese words for bat and
unicorn are homonymous with "fortune" and "longevity,"
hence its auspicious message.

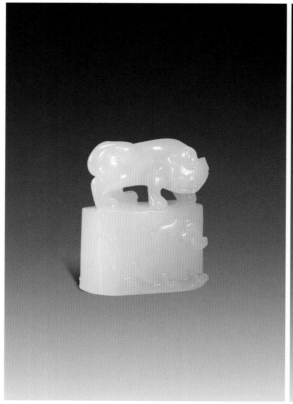

白玉凤鸟钮双联印

清
高 4.2厘米   长 2.9厘米

　　白玉质，玉质洁白无瑕。两个长方形小玉印并排联在一起，印顶部呈盝顶形，大小基本相同。玉印之上的钮由一大一小两只凤鸟组成。凤的形体较大，圆眼，脑后有长长的卷毛，身饰短翼，长尾弯卷于身下，并以绞丝纹来表示。鸟似鹦鹉，回首，与凤四目相对，立于凤的背上，圆眼，尖喙呈钩状，尾弯卷抵于喙部。羽翼及细部花纹均以阴刻线刻划。此双联印选料考究，精雕细琢，为清代玉印中的佳作。

White jade twin seals with knob in the shape of phoenix and bird

Qing Dynasty (1644~1911)
Height 4.2cm   Length 2.9cm

　　The two small rectangular seals are carved in crystal clear white jade. The top of the seals, similar sized, are shaped like low cubes. The knob of the seals is a carved phoenix and a bird. The phoenix is larger, with round eyes and long curled feathers at the back of its head. On its body are engraved lines showing short wings. Its long tail curls down its body. The tail is presented with curved lines. The other bird, in the shape of a parrot standing on its back, turns its head to look into the eyes of the phoenix. Its eyes are round and its beak is hooked. Its tail bends towards its beak. The designs of its feathers and wings are presented with incised lines. The twin seals are fine pieces cut during the Qing Dynasty.

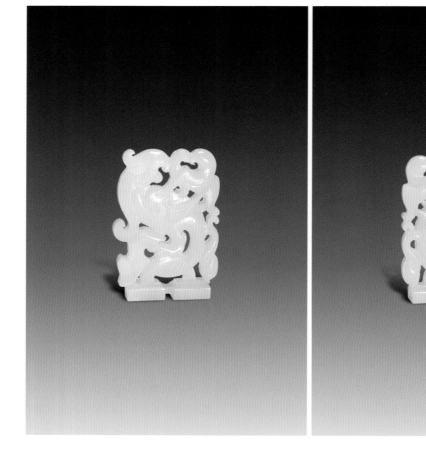

40

白玉莲蝠纹印盒

清
高 3.5厘米　径 5.7厘米 × 5.7厘米

　　白玉质，有自然沁色。印盒为子母口。盒盖四
边留窄棱，采用减地平钑和阴刻线相结合的雕琢方
法，表现两只蝙蝠展翅飞翔在祥云中，一支莲花挺
立于山水之间。盒腹较深，底部四角各有一曲尺形
足。整体造型简洁，纹饰流畅自然，琢磨精湛，是
书房中精致的雅玩小品。

White jade seal box with lotus and bat design

Qing Dynasty (1644~1911)
Height 3.5cm　Diameter 5.7cm×5.7cm

　　The box is made of jade with signs of natural oozing
over time. The lid, with a narrow edge, can be inserted into
the double-rimmed mouth. Cut by removing part of the
surface and incision, the two bats spreading their wings are
set among auspicious clouds. A lotus is presented against
a landscape. The box is deep and at the four corners of its
bottom are four feet. The whole box is concisely composed
and finely polished, decorated with flowing lines. It is an
elegant contrivance for a scholar's study.

41

白玉兽面纹剑格

清
高 2.1厘米　长 5.2厘米

　　白玉质，玉质细腻。剑格上端呈凹字形，下端呈三角形，截面为菱形。两面均饰兽面纹，兽面凸眼、粗眉，眉毛以阴刻线表示。兽面两侧饰隐起的勾云纹，纹饰对称。中部有用以置剑柄的穿孔。

　　剑格也称护手，它是镶嵌于剑柄与剑身交接处的饰物。以玉饰剑的风气盛行于春秋战国至两汉时期，此件玉剑格为清代仿古作品。

White jade sword *Ge* with animal face design

Qing Dynasty (1644~1911)
Height 2.1cm　Length 5.2cm

　　This sword *Ge* has a notched top and triangular bottom. Its horizontal cross-section is a rhombus. Both sides are ornamented with animal faces with protruding eyes and incised dense eyebrows. By both sides of the animal faces are faintly visible symmetrical designs of cirrus. The hole for the sword handle runs through the middle.

　　Jade was widely used to decorate swords, from the late 8th century BC to the early 3rd century AD. This hand guard is a Qing-dynasty copy of an ancient hand guard.

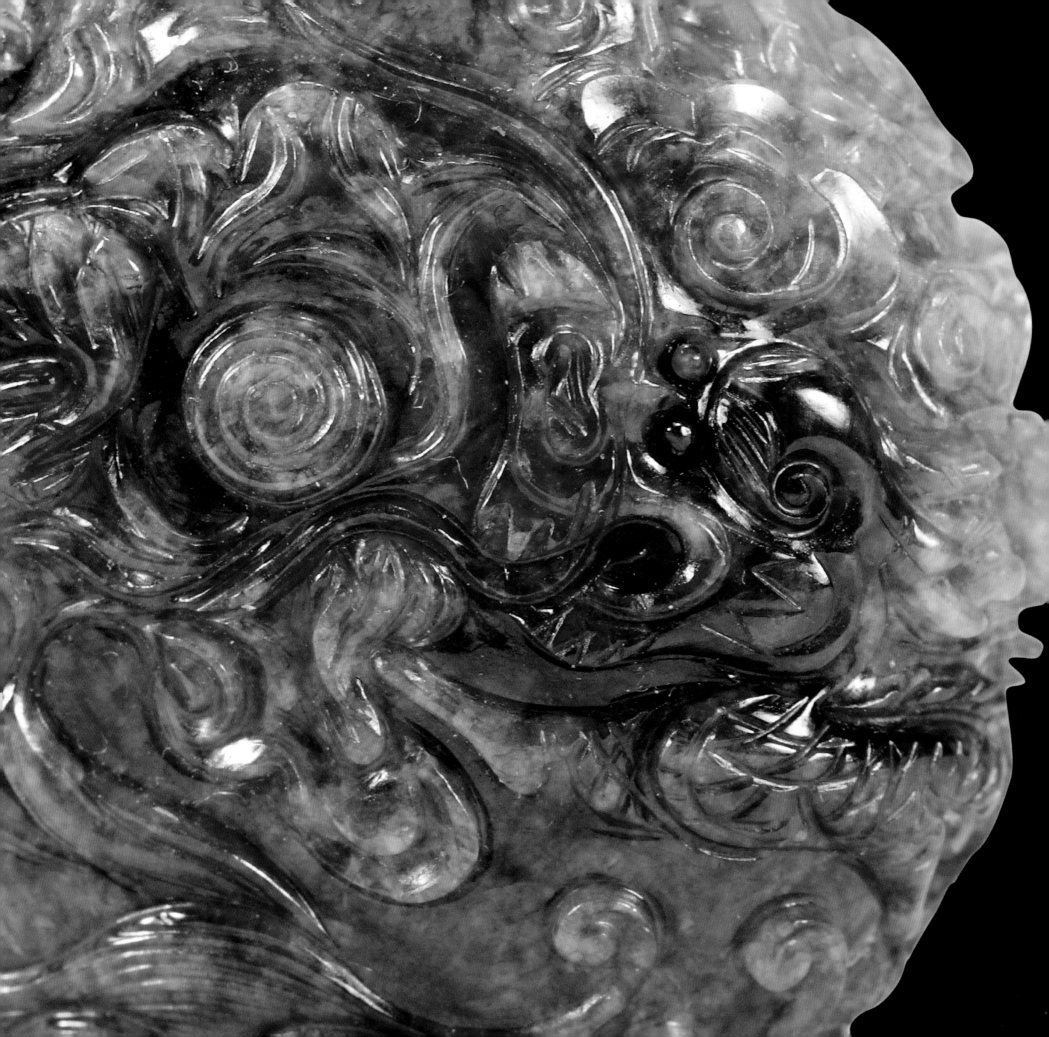

鼻烟壶篇 Snuff bottle

玻璃胎画珐琅开光西洋山水人物图鼻烟壶

清乾隆
通高 4.6厘米　宽 3厘米

　　錾花铜鎏金盖，扁圆形壶身，玻璃胎画珐琅。壶身两面开光，其上绘胭脂粉色西洋建筑、风景和人物。所绘内容充分体现了画家精湛的技艺，画面有明暗处理，可以看出是西方绘画的方法，底足内有阴刻"乾隆年制"四字楷书款，是典型的乾隆时期宫廷代表作。绘制精美，色彩清新淡雅。

Glass snuff bottle with European landscape and human figures design painted with enamel

Qianlong Reign (1736~1795), Qing Dynasty
Overall height 4.6cm　Width 3cm

　　This glass bottle with an enamel coating has a gilded copper lid. This flat, circular bottle has bordered pictures on its front and back. Within its borders are landscapes, European-style buildings and figure, painted in rose hues. The paintings exhibit the artist's exquisite skill in using light and shade as displayed in European painting. On the bottom is an inscription engraved in regular script, reading, "Made in the Qianlong Reign." A typical product from the imperial court during the Qianlong Reign, the bottle is noted for its beautiful painting, and refreshing, graceful colours.

玻璃胎画珐琅花蝶纹鼻烟壶

清
通高 6.8厘米　宽 4.1厘米

　　碧玺盖，葫芦形壶身，黄色胎体，不透明，玻璃胎画珐琅。周身绘满花卉及蝴蝶、蜻蜓纹饰，画工精致细腻，生动逼真。底足内书"古月轩"款。进口颜料，烧制复杂。整体造型工整，色泽温润。

Glass snuff bottle with enamel design of butterflies

Qing Dynasty (1644~1911)
Overall height 6.8cm　　Width 4.1cm

　　This glass bottle with an enamel coating in the shape of a gourd has a tourmaline lid. The body, in opaque yellow glass, is covered with designs of flowers, butterflies, dragonflies, and other insects. The flowers are meticulously painted, with the butterflies and dragonflies vivid and lifelike. On the bottom is the inscription, "Gu Yue Studio." Imported pigments were used to paint the bottle. The process of firing this bottle was very complicated. The bottle is in a regular form, and its colouring is warm and moderate.

白套粉玻璃牧牛图鼻烟壶

清中期
通高 7.4厘米　宽 3.3厘米

　　翡翠盖，瓶形壶身，涅白地玻璃胎套粉红色玻璃。壶身一面雕驾舟采荷图，上方刻"十里采荷"四字；另一面雕牧童放牛图，旁边刻有"吉羊"二字边款，寓意吉祥如意。壶两侧还雕有兽面环耳。该作品色泽素雅可人，整体布局得当，雕工细致，具有典型的清中期扬州工艺特点。

White glass snuff bottle with carved lotus gatherer and cowherd in rose glass

Mid-Qing Dynasty
Overall height 7.4cm　Width 3.3cm

　　The bottle in opaque white glass has a lid made of jadeite. It is decorated with red glass designs. On its front is the carving of two people coasting on a boat and gathering lotus flowers, with the inscription, "sweet lotus flowers over ten li." On the other side is the carving of a cowherd, with a colophon *Jiyang* (auspice). On the side of the bottle are small handles decorated with carved animal faces. The colouring is light and graceful, and the composition is tranquil. This meticulously carved bottle was produced in Yangzhou during the middle of the Qing Dynasty.

白套红玻璃四灵图鼻烟壶

清
通高 6.7厘米　宽 4.9厘米

　　珊瑚盖，银托，扁圆形壶身，珍珠泡地（俗称：
唾沫地）玻璃胎套红色玻璃。壶身雕有四灵：麟、
凤、龟、龙，古人将他们视为吉祥瑞兽，孔颖达疏：
"神灵之鸟兽，王者之嘉瑞也。"套红玻璃较厚，琢
磨出的四灵形象起伏较高，类似起凸雕法，图案布
局繁密，雕刻手法娴熟，形态栩栩如生。

White glass snuff bottle with pattern of four mythical creatures on red glass

Qing Dynasty (1644~1911)
Overall height 6.7cm　Width 4.9cm

　　With a lid of coral, the bottle has a base of white
glass with bubbles in it. A part of it is covered with red
glass sculpted with designs of mythical creatures: a *Qilin*,
a phoenix, a turtle and a dragon. It was believed that these
creatures were fortuitous signs for the ruler of a country.
The red glass on top of the white base is thick. The
composition is tight, and the creatures are lifelike.

白套绿玻璃梅花纹鼻烟壶

清中期
通高 7.4厘米　宽 3.5厘米

　　珊瑚盖，瓶形壶身，珍珠地玻璃胎套绿色玻璃。该作品以梅花为题材，壶身通体雕刻带枝梅花，底部雕有一整朵梅花作为底座，可谓设计巧妙，雕工亦极为精细。梅花向来被古人所推崇，因其品格高尚，傲然绽放。总体来说涅白地衬托的亮绿梅花图案鲜亮醒目，清新素雅。

White glass snuff bottle with plum blossom design on green glass

Mid-Qing Dynasty
Overall height 7.4cm　Width 3.5cm

　　The bottle, with a base of pale greyish white glass, has plum blossoms carved on green glass. Its lid is made of coral. The plum blossom, a favoured image in ancient Chinese art, is praised for its courage to brave the cold in winter. While plum blossom branches cover the whole bottle, the bottom of the bottle bears a single sculpted plum flower. The bottle is ingeniously conceived and meticulous carved. Against an opaque white background, the brilliant green blossom is eye-catching.

47

白套蓝玻璃麒麟龙纹鼻烟壶

清
通高 6.1厘米　宽 4.4厘米

　　碧玺盖，扁圆形壶身，透明珍珠地玻璃胎套蓝色玻璃。壶身一面雕麒麟；另一面雕龙纹。麒麟和龙都被古人视为瑞兽，寓意吉祥。此壶上的纹饰形象写意，采用凸雕手法，图案布局疏朗简洁，主题纹饰醒目突出，具有很高的欣赏价值。

White glass snuff bottle with design of *Qilin* and dragon on blue glass

Qing Dynasty (1644~1911)
Overall height 6.1cm　Width 4.4cm

　　Made of opaque white glass, the flat and round bottle with a tourmaline lid bears reliefs in blue glass. On one side of the bottle is a mythical animal *Qilin* and on the other side is a dragon. Both the *Qilin* and dragon have been regarded as auspicious animals since ancient times. The relief on the bottle is sketchily executed and sparsely arranged, a composition that sets off the main motifs. The bottle is of high artistic value.

48

白套双色玻璃博古图鼻烟壶

清
通高 7厘米　宽 3.1厘米

　　碧玺盖，瓶形壶身，乳白色玻璃胎，复套蓝、粉双色玻璃。壶身两面雕刻博古纹。在器身上先套蓝色玻璃，其上再套粉色玻璃，复套工艺复杂，色泽淡雅，构思别致，具有极强的立体感。

White glass snuff bottle with pattern of antiques on blue and pink glass

Qing Dynasty (1644~1911)
Overall height 7cm　Width 3.1cm

　　The creamy white glass bottle has a lid of apyrite. The front and back of the bottle are decorated with blue and pink glass designs of antique objects. A blue glass coating was applied beneath the pink coating – a complex technical process. In light, graceful colours, the ingeniously conceived bottle gives off a strong three-dimensional visual effect.

49

白套五彩玻璃松鹤鸳鸯纹鼻烟壶

清中期
通高 5.9厘米　宽 4.3厘米

　　珊瑚盖，扁圆形壶身，乳白色玻璃胎，上套粉、绿、蓝、黄、褐五色玻璃。壶身两面分别雕刻"荷花鸳鸯"、"松鹤长春"图纹，套玻璃雕工精细，画面生动传神，色彩雅致，为典型的扬州工艺。

White glass snuff bottle with design of lotus, mandarin ducks, pine and cranes in five colours

Mid-Qing Dynasty
Overall height 5.9cm　Width 4.3cm

　　This bottle, with a base of creamy white glass, has a lid of coral. With carved designs of lotus flowers, mandarin ducks, pine and cranes in rose, green, blue, yellow and ochre glass, the flat round bottle has been meticulously executed. The vivid images in light, graceful colours are a hallmark of snuff bottles produced in Yangzhou.

50

白套六彩玻璃瓜果纹鼻烟壶

清
通高 7.1厘米　宽 4厘米

　　碧玺盖，扁瓶形壶身，透明珍珠地玻璃胎，上套红、黄、粉、绿、湖蓝、肝红六色玻璃。缠枝瓜果纹雕满壶身，瓜果或红、或黄、或粉、或绿、或湖蓝、或肝红，随意套彩，色泽清新雅丽，雕工精美，造型典雅秀丽。

White glass snuff bottle with design of melon and fruit in six colours

Qing Dynasty (1644~1911)
Overall height 7.1cm　Width 4cm

　　This transparent white glass bottle with apyrite lid has designs of fruit and winding vines carved in red, rose, yellow, blue and brown glass. The brilliant colour and fine carving set off the elegance of the bottle.

白套六彩玻璃官上加官图鼻烟壶

清
通高 7.8厘米　宽 4.2厘米

　　碧玺盖，瓶形壶身，珍珠泡地玻璃胎，上套红、黄、绿、蓝、粉、黑六色玻璃。壶身雕刻公鸡、鸡冠花，取"冠"与"官"谐音，寓意"官上加官"。图案生动活泼，套色之多极为罕见，工艺非常复杂，制作上体现出极高的水准。

White glass snuff bottle with design of rooster and cockscomb in six colours

Qing Dynasty (1644~1911)
Overall height 7.8cm　Width 4.2cm

　　The bottle in opaque white glass has apyrite lid, and is covered with red, yellow, green, blue, rose and black glass. Roosters and cockscombs are carved on the bottle. A rooster with a "*guan*" (crest) on top of its head is under a flower called "*ji guan*" (cockscomb), which together play on the Chinese phrase "*guan shang jia guan*" – one official position after another, implying continual promotion in rank. The lively images and excellent use of coloured glass in the bottle reveal superb technique.

藕粉地套四色玻璃花蝶纹鼻烟壶

清乾隆
通高 5.2厘米　宽 3.7厘米

　　螭虎纹绿料盖，扁圆形壶身，藕粉色玻璃胎套红、姜黄、蓝、绿四色玻璃。壶身两面各雕刻一朵缠枝花，两侧肩部各雕一只蝴蝶。整体图案布局规整，线条流畅，雕工精细。

Snuff bottle in pale pinkish purple glass with flower and butterfly design in four colours

Qianlong Reign (1736~1795), Qing Dynasty
Overall height 5.2cm　Width 3.7cm

　　This flat and circular snuff bottle is covered with red, yellow, blue and green glass. It has a green glass lid with the engraved design of a *Chi*-dragon. On its front is a lotus flower with winding vines, as on its back. Each of its left and right sides has a butterfly. The overall design of the bottle is regular, and the decoration is executed in flowing lines.

柠檬黄玻璃胎鼻烟壶

清中期
通高 6.4厘米　宽 4.4厘米

　　碧玺盖，瓜棱形壶身，柠檬黄色玻璃胎。烟壶造型周正，磨制细腻，线条的表现极为突出，体现出乾隆时期工艺特点，色泽淡雅，实为佳作。

Yellow glass snuff bottle

Mid-Qing Dynasty
Overall height 6.4cm　Width 4.4cm

　　The bottle is made of lemon yellow glass with apyrite lid. The body of the bottle is in the shape of a pumpkin, a hallmark of Qianlong-era artefacts. The shape of the bottle is prominently linear. Its superior shape, light colour and fine polish contribute to the beauty of the bottle.

玻璃胎诸葛亮肖像内画鼻烟壶

清
通高 7.2厘米　宽 3.8厘米

蟠螭纹珊瑚盖，扁瓶形壶身，玻璃胎。壶身一面绘诸葛亮的舞台形象，羽扇纶巾，睿智儒雅；另一面题诗一首："云霞白书孤鹤，风雨深山卧龙，闭户追思古典，著述已足三分。"旁题："乙巳六月，马少宣。"

马少宣是清末京派内画四大画师之一，其内画鼻烟壶书画并茂、笔法精湛，"一面诗一面画"是其内画鼻烟壶最常见的装饰形式，内画题材尤以人物肖像擅长，所绘人物肖像善于用若明若暗的浅墨色调，形象、神韵栩栩如生。

Glass snuff bottle with portrait of Zhuge Liang painted on the inner side

Qing Dynasty (1644~1911)
Overall height 7.2cm　Width 3.8cm

The flat snuff bottle has a coral lid with patterns of a *Chi*-dragon has the portrait of the ancient mastermind Zhuge Liang painted on the inner side of its wall. Zhuge Liang appears insightful and composed, with a feather fan in hand, as he is presented on stage. On the other side of the bottle is the inscription of a poem: "Like a solitary crane flying in clouds on the day; / Or a dragon lying in wind and rain in deep mountains, / He shuts himself in his study to mull over the past. / His works contain strategies for government of a third of the world." The colophon reads, "Ma Shaoxuan, in the Year of Yisi". The year of Yisi was 1905.

Ma Shaoxuan (1867~1939) was one of the four leading painters of inside-painted snuff bottles in Beijing at the end of the Qing Dynasty. Snuff bottles painted by him are noted for concise brushwork. Snuff bottles painted by him usually had a painting on one side and a poem on the other. He triumphed in lifelike portraits, which was executed with light ink.

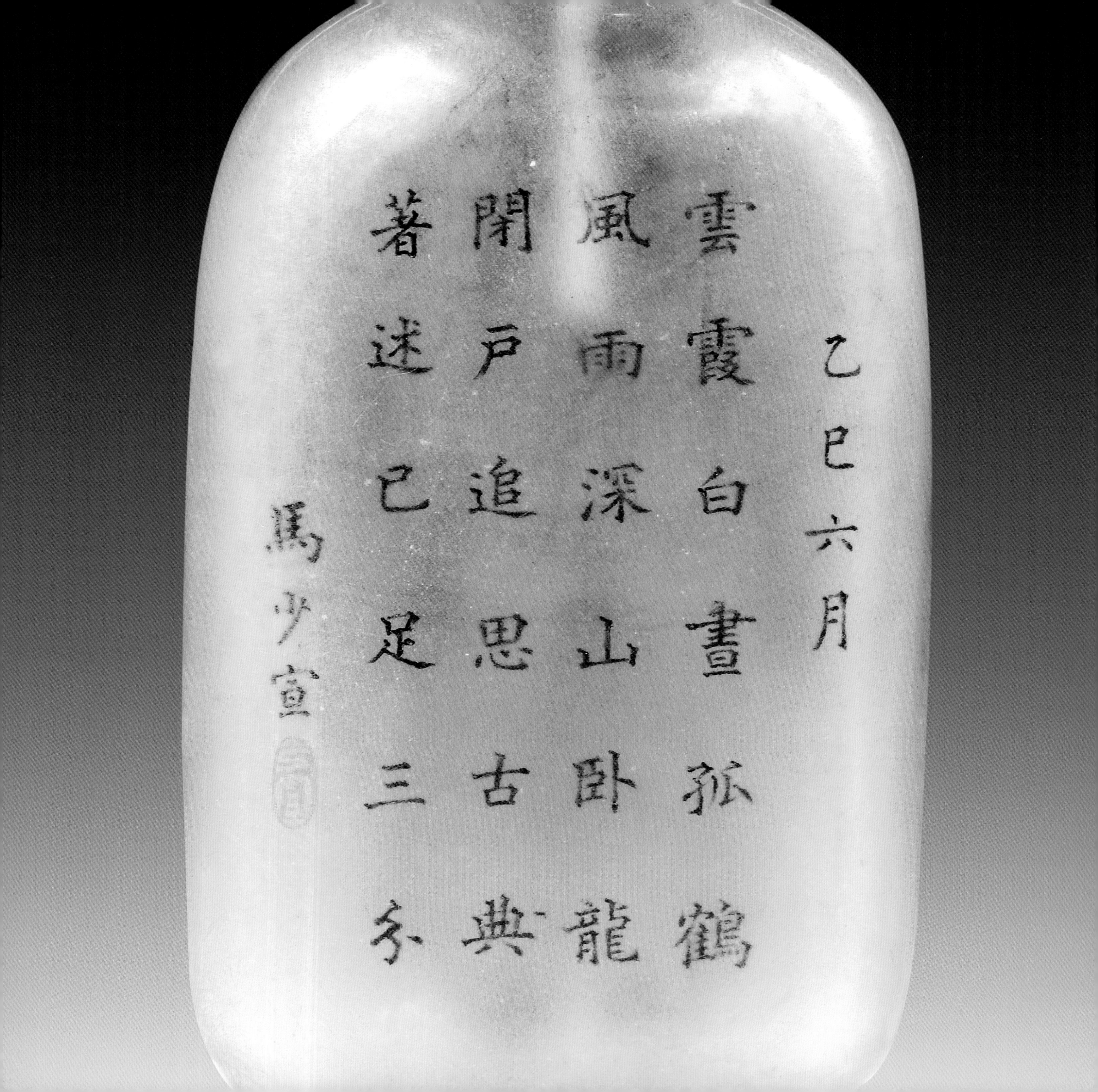

乙巳六月

雲霞白晝孤鶴
風雨深山臥龍
閑戶追思古典
著述已足三分

馬少宣〔印〕

白玉折方式鼻烟壶

清乾隆
通高 6.7厘米　宽 4.1厘米

　　翡翠盖，折方式壶身，羊脂白玉质。此件作品光素无纹，遵循"良材不雕"的古制，通体不着一刀，以利表现玉质。作品以线条取胜，造型规整，典雅，玉质纯净光润，由一块籽料雕刻而成。为乾隆时期典型佳作。

White jade oblong snuff bottle

Qianlong Reign (1736~1795), Qing Dynasty
Overall height 6.7cm　Width 4.1cm

　　Cut from a nugget of smooth and fine jade, this bottle with an jadeite lid has no decoration. A plain object sets off good quality jade, as the old adage goes, "Good material need not to be carved." The bottle, noted for its graceful shape and pure and clear material, was produced during the Qianlong reign of the Qing Dynasty.

白玉鼻烟壶

清中期
通高 6.2厘米　宽 4.8厘米

　　珊瑚盖，扁圆形壶身，白玉质。素鼻烟壶在选料和碾琢上要求很高，这件作品通体光素无纹，玉质纯净无瑕，细腻莹润，色彩均匀，以上等的和田籽料雕刻而成，器表光滑，器形端正饱满。

White jade snuff bottle

Mid-Qing Dynasty
Overall height 6.2cm　Width 4.8cm

　　This flat and circular bottle has a lid of coral. It is an exacting task to produce a plain snuff bottle. The jade must be free from any impurity, while the colour should be even, and the surface smooth. This plain bottle is carved from first-rate jade from Khotan, Xinjiang.

白玉喜报平安图鼻烟壶

清中期
通高 6.1厘米　宽 4.4厘米

　　碧玺盖，扁圆形壶身，白玉质。壶身以文字做主题装饰，圆形为限，巧分而琢。两面分别雕有"喜报"和"平安"，乃为"喜报平安"之意，是当时常用的吉祥语，起地阳文，字体打挖，非常精美。整件作品质地温润，由一块和田籽料整体雕刻而成，线条流畅。

White jade snuff bottle with inscriptions of "happy tidings" and "peace"

Mid-Qing Dynasty
Overall height 6.1cm　Width 4.4cm

　　The flat and round bottle, with its lid of apyrite, bears inscriptions on both sides, "Happy Tidings" and "Peace," which are common blessings. The inscriptions are cut in relief. Cut from a nugget of smooth jade from Khotan, Xinjiang, the bottle has a very graceful form.

白玉梅花诗文鼻烟壶

清中期
通高 6厘米　宽 4.5厘米

　　珊瑚盖，扁圆形壶身，白玉质。壶身一面阴刻有明代高启《梅花九首》中的诗句"秦人若解当时种，不引渔郎入洞天"，另一面在玉皮处巧妙的阴刻几朵梅花。展现了"俏色"工艺的独特风采。玉质细腻温润，由一块和田籽料雕刻而成。

White jade snuff bottle with incised plum blossoms and inscribed poem

Mid-Qing Dynasty
Overall height 6cm　Width 4.5cm

　　This flat and round bottle has a lid of coral. On its front are lines engraved from Gao Qi's poem on plum blossoms, "If Qin people knew to plant plum trees, fishermen would not be lured to a distant river source." These lines refer to a tale of fifth century fishermen who saw a forest of peach trees blooming, without any other trees, and in their attempt to find the end of the forest they traced the stream to its source, where they came across people who had arrived there 700 years before, who had no idea what happened after their ancestors had arrived at the source of the river. On the snuff bottle's back are several plum blossoms, lent their colour by the surface of the jade. The smooth, fine jade used was produced in Khotan, Xinjiang.

白玉葫芦形鼻烟壶

清
通高 6.2厘米　宽 3.7厘米

　　碧玺盖，上嵌珍珠，葫芦形壶身，白玉质。葫芦取"福禄"的谐音，寓意吉祥。玉质细腻温润。烟壶整体造型优美，比例协调。在壶身两侧通体各雕刻出一束洋莲，细腰处镶嵌了一圈红宝石，具有痕都斯坦风格，使整个作品看上去象一位贵妇人雍容华贵。

White jade snuff bottle in the shape of calabash

Qing Dynasty (1644~1911)
Overall height 6.2cm　Width 3.7cm

　　With an apyrite lid, the snuff bottle made of white jade is in the shape of a calabash. The name of the calabash in Chinese is homonymous with the phrase "fortune and wealth", hence an auspicious sign. The well-proportioned bottle is graceful. On the left and right sides of the bottle are carved a bunch of dahlias and at the waist of the bottle is a ring of rubies, which is an earmark of Hindustan style. The whole bottle looks as graceful and majestic as a noblewoman. The jade used is fine and smooth.

60

白玉茄式鼻烟壶

清
通高 6.1厘米　宽 2厘米

茄柄式碧玉盖，以碧玉雕茄蒂，白玉示茄身。造型优美生动，二者完美地结合在一起。玉质细腻，由和田籽料雕刻而成。

White jade snuff bottle in shape of aubergine

Qing Dynasty (1644~1911)
Overall height 6.1cm　Width 2cm

The snuff bottle is carved from a whole nugget of fine and smooth white jade. The bottle takes on the shape of an aubergine. The mouth of the bottle is stopped with a jasper lid that is carved into the shape of the handle of the aubergine. The lid and the bottle match perfectly.

61

白玉四季花卉纹鼻烟壶

清
通高6.1厘米　宽4厘米

　　碧玺盖，扁圆形壶身，白玉质。壶身两面浮雕
梅、兰、竹、菊四季花卉，雕工精细，线条流畅，
玉质纯净。

White jade snuff bottle with flower design

Qing Dynasty (1644~1911)
Overall height 6.1cm　　Width 4cm

　　The flat and circular white jade bottle with a lid
of apyrite has reliefs of plum, orchid, bamboo, and
chrysanthemum flowers. The bottle in pure jade is noted
for its free and flowing cutting.

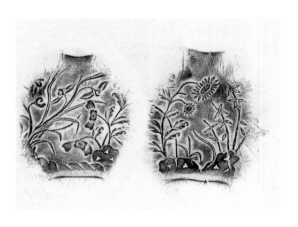

白玉三狮戏球图鼻烟壶

清
通高 6.8厘米　宽 4.8厘米

　　珊瑚盖，扁圆形壶身，白玉质。壶身上雕狮子戏球图案。雕工精致，线条细致流畅，玉质纯净光润，由一整块籽料雕刻而成。

White jade snuff bottle with design of three lions playing with ball

Qing Dynasty (1644~1911)
Overall height 6.8cm　Width 4.8cm

　　This flat and round bottle has jade body with a lid of coral. On the bottle, three lions are carved playing with a ball. The carving is smooth and meticulous. The whole bottle is cut from a nugget of crystal clear, fine jade.

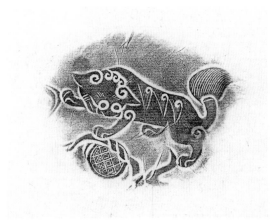

青白玉渔樵耕读图鼻烟壶

清
通高 7.2厘米　宽 4.6厘米

　　绿晶石盖，方瓶形壶身，青白玉质。壶身的一面利用玉皮凸雕出渔樵耕读图，另一面光素无纹，两侧各雕有衔环兽面，雕刻栩栩如生，充分展示了"俏色"的独特工艺。

Greenish-white jade snuff bottle with design of a fisherman, a farmer's cow, a woodcutter and a scholar

Qing Dynasty (1644~1911)
Overall height 7.2cm　Width 4.6cm

　　The oblong bottle has a creature's face holding a ring in its mouth on each of the two sides, and on its body are depicted a fisherman, a farmer's cow, a woodcutter and a scholar, all cut in relief. The depiction is vivid and lifelike, and the hues of the original surface of the stone are cleverly employed.

青白玉百宝嵌花鸟人物图鼻烟壶

清
通高 6.3厘米　宽 3.6厘米

　　碧玺盖，瓶形壶身，青白玉质。玉质壶身上镶有珊瑚、象牙等材质雕刻的花鸟人物，镶嵌方式吸取了外来文化的特点，图案生动传神，构思巧妙，别具匠心。

Greenish-white jade snuff bottle with pattern of a bird, flowers and human figures

Qing Dynasty (1644~1911)
Overall height 6.3cm　Width 3.6cm

　　The flat snuff bottle made of greenish-white jade is covered with an apyrite lid. This bottle is embedded with designs of birds, flowers and human figures carved from coral and ivory. The method of embedding draws on foreign art. The designs are vivid and lifelike, as well as ingeniously conceived. The material used is fine and smooth.

墨玉龙狮纹鼻烟壶

清
通高 9.6厘米　宽 6.2厘米

　　珊瑚盖，扁瓶形壶身，墨玉质。壶身一面雕刻"苍龙教子"图，苍龙腾空而起，虬躯矫健凶猛，幼龙则破浪而出，昂首欲飞，雕刻生动精美，表达了望子成才的愿望；另一面雕刻"三狮嬉戏"图，雄狮威武雄壮，形神俱佳，幼狮活泼可爱，栩栩如生，以细腻的雕刻传示出浓浓的殷切之情。整件作品由一块墨玉雕刻而成。其雕刻工艺具有典型的"苏州工"特点。

Black jade snuff bottle with design of dragon and lion

Qing Dynasty (1644~1911)
Overall height 9.6cm　Width 6.2cm

　　The flat snuff bottle made of black jade is covered with a coral lid. On one side of the bottle is carved a dragon training his son. The old dragon soaring into the air looks powerful and dignified while the young dragon leaps up from waves. The precise and lifelike carving conveys a message that everyone hopes his son to be a "dragon" (a successful man). On the other side of the bottle are carved three playing lions. The large lion looks awe-inspiring while the lion cubs lively. The whole bottle is carved from a block of black jade. The carving partakes of Suzhou artisans' style.

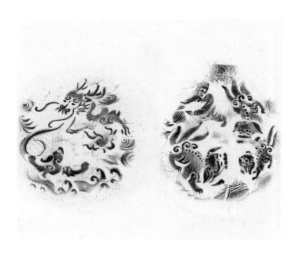

翡翠海水龙纹鼻烟壶

清
通高 7.1厘米　宽 5厘米

　　碧玺盖，银鎏金托，扁瓶形壶身，翡翠质。壶身满雕不留地，两面雕刻组成一幅图案，一条龙穿行于福海的波涛汹涌之中。龙雕刻的气宇轩昂，风生水起，海水浪花布满壶身，跳跃灵动，手法细腻而娴熟。翡翠颜色属于艳绿色，浓艳、色正。

Jadeite snuff bottle with design of dragon in seawater

Qing Dynasty (1644~1911)
Overall height 7.1cm　Width 5cm

　　With a apyrite lid, the flat snuff bottle made of jadeite has a carved dragon swimming in a raging sea. The imposing dragon stirs up billows which cover the bottle all over. The carving is consummately executed. The emerald is brilliantly green, which is the colour of top-quality jadeite.

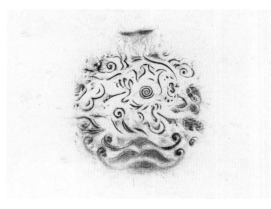

玛瑙花鸟人物诗文鼻烟壶

清中期
通高 5.7厘米　宽 4厘米

　　碧玺盖，扁圆形壶身，玛瑙质。壶身周身利用俏色巧作花鸟人物纹饰，并用阳文刻有陶渊明《归去来辞》中的"松菊犹存"四字。玛瑙上刻文字难度较大，容易走砣而影响其神韵，而这件作品的文字雕刻流畅、精细，俏色的运用娴熟，体现出很高的工艺水平。

Agate snuff bottle with design of bird, flower and human figure and inscription of a poem

Mid-Qing Dynasty
Overall height 5.7cm　Width 4cm

　　This flat and round agate bottle has a apyrite lid. On its body are designs of birds, flowers and human figures, carved using the original hues of the surface of the agate. Further, an inscription is carved in relief, reading "Pine and chrysanthemum still remain," a line from Tao Yuanming's poetic prose, "On His Going Home." Tao Yuanming, living in the fourth and fifth centuries, was a poet who resigned from officialdom and became a hermit. The carving out of characters on agate is a difficult task, since the knife tends to slip and damage any image being produced. The characters on this bottle, however, are precise and fluent, and the colours of the original surface are ingeniously employed. All these point to the artisan's superb skill.

玛瑙李白醉酒诗文鼻烟壶

清中期
通高 7.2厘米　宽 4.9厘米

　　珊瑚盖，圆形壶身，玛瑙质。烟壶周身环刻
"李白醉酒赋诗"意境，并刻有诗文，一面阳刻
"李白一斗诗百篇"，另一面阴刻"自称臣是酒中
仙"。整件作品具有典型的苏作风格，山石流水间
带着动感，以山石为周底，展开是一幅整体图案，
平底。俏色工艺运用巧妙，繁而不乱。

Agate snuff bottle depicting a drunk poet

Mid-Qing Dynasty
Overall height 7.2cm　Width 4.9cm

　　he round agate bottle has a lid of coral. On the
surface of the bottle is carved a portrayal of the poet Li
Bai drinking and composing poems, against mountains
and flowing water, giving the feeling of movement. On
one side is a line cut in relief, reading, "With a vat of wine
down, Li Bai chants a hundred poems"; and on the other
side, the engraved line, "He claims he is an immortal
drunkard" (these two lines are from a poem from a
contemporary, describing how the drunk Li Bai wrote to
belittle the emperor). The bottle is a Suzhou product. The
colouring on the original surface of the agate is cleverly
used, and the composition among the many objects is
finely arranged.

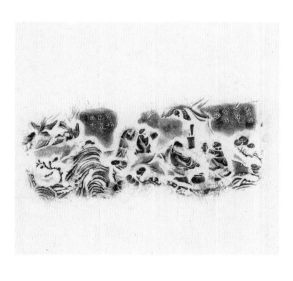

玛瑙西番莲纹鼻烟壶

清
通高 6.5厘米　宽 4.9厘米

　　珊瑚盖，扁圆形壶身，玛瑙质。烟壶两面各雕刻一朵西番莲，纹饰布局错落有致，雕刻细腻圆润，线条流畅自然，整幅图案活泼而不失严谨，具有极强的装饰趣味，体现出很高的工艺水平。

Agate snuff bottle with engraved dahlia design

Qing Dynasty(1644~1911)
Overall height 6.5cm　Width 4.9cm

　　The flat and round snuff bottle with a coral lid has a dahlia on each of its two sides. The carving is executed in smooth line. The rhythmically arranged pattern is both precise and full of life. The highly decorative bottle exhibits superb craftsmanship.

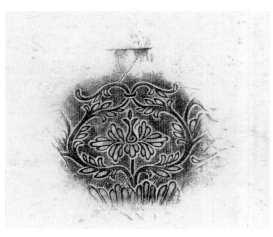

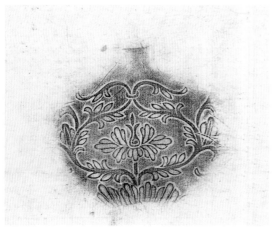

玛瑙马到功成图鼻烟壶

清
通高 7.1厘米　宽 5厘米

　　珊瑚盖，方瓶形壶身，玛瑙质。壶身一面雕刻
一个栓马桩，上面拴着一匹千里马，寓意"马到功
成"，在雕刻中巧妙的运用了俏色工艺，使纹饰形象
生动传神；另一面通体光素无纹。整体给人一种动
静结合，相得益彰之感。

Agate snuff bottle with horse design

Qing Dynasty (1644~1911)
Overall height 7.1cm　Width 5cm

　　The square agate bottle has a lid of coral. On its
one side, the oblong snuff bottle with a coral lid has the
sculpture of a winged steed tied to a post. The motif
is synonymous with the Chinese phrase for "instant
success". Original colour of the material is cleverly
used to present part of the horse. The other side of the
bottle is plain. The patterns on the bottle make a union of
movement and stillness.

水晶百寿纹鼻烟壶

清早期
通高 7.1厘米　宽 3.9厘米

　　蟠螭纹珊瑚盖，扁瓶形壶身，水晶质。壶身通体浮雕团寿字，取圆形造型，凸起上阴刻"寿"字，布局规整，质地优良，碾琢精细。

　　水晶古称水玉，又名水精。硬度很高，性脆，琢磨纹饰不易。

Crystal snuff bottle with 100 characters for "Longevity"

Early Qing Dynasty
Overall height 7.1cm　Width 3.9cm

　　The crystal bottle has a lid of coral carved into a *Chi-dragon*. *The body of* the bottle is covered with circularized characters for *Shou*, meaning "longevity." This bottle bears regularly arranged characters, and is finely polished.

　　In ancient times,crystal once has the name of "water jade"(*shuijing*) or "water spirit" (*shuijing*). Crystal is hard and brittle and it is difficult to cut designs on it.

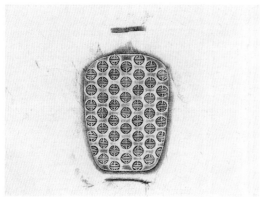

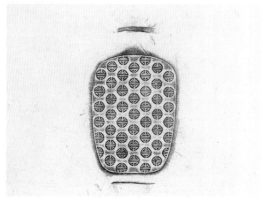

水晶人物故事图内画鼻烟壶

清
通高 7.5厘米　宽 4.4厘米

　　蟠螭纹玻璃盖，扁瓶形壶身，水晶质。壶身一面绘二位高士和一位高僧围坐在松下石桌旁品茗清谈，题材高雅，人物形象生动；另一面描绘了雪中送故人，图中一对男女在江边树下送别一位骑驴老者，人物神采奕奕，衣服色彩鲜明，旁题："丁酉腊月作于京师　叶仲三。"

　　叶仲三是清末的内画鼻烟壶大师。他的内画作品以雅俗共赏著称于世。特别擅于历史人物和民间传说的题材，对人物的神态刻意求工，栩栩如生，被称为内画人物一绝。

Crystal snuff bottle with figures painted on the inner wall

Qing Dynasty (1644~1911)
Overall height 7.5cm　Width 4.4cm

With a glass lid cut into the shape of a *Chi*-dragon, the flat crystal snuff bottle has the inner side of its wall painted. The painting on one of its sides shows the life-like images of two scholars and a Buddhist monk chatting and drinking tea at a stone table. On the other side of the bottle is a couple bidding farewell to an old man riding a donkey under a tree by a river, against snow-covered landscape. The human figures in brilliant costume are brimming with vitality. The inscription reads, "By Ye Zhongsan, in the capital, the twelfth moon of the year of Dingyou". The year of Dingyou was 1897.

A master hand in painting the inner wall of snuff bottles at the end of the Qing Dynasty, Ye Zhongsan excelled in themes of historical story and folk literature. His works pleasing high-brows and low-brows alike have been praised for vivid and precise images.

琥珀折方式鼻烟壶

清乾隆
通高 7.2厘米　宽 4.1厘米

　　青金石盖，折方式壶身，呈棕红色，琥珀质。通体光素无纹，胎体透明、纯净、无杂质。天然纹理在光线照射下显得晶莹剔透、莹澈可爱，内部掏空规整，琢磨规矩精细，是典型的乾隆时期作品。

　　琥珀是数千万年前的树脂被埋藏地下，经过一定化学变化后形成的一种树脂化石。

Amber oblong snuff bottle

Qianlong Reign (1736~1795), Qing Dynasty
Overall height 7.2cm　Width 4.1cm

　　This bottle in reddish brown amber has a lazurite lid. The oblong bottle is not embellished at all, which sets off the transparency and purity of the material used. Against light, the natural veins of the amber are clearly visible. The interior is smoothly hollowed and finely polished. It is a typical work of the Qianlong reign in the Qing Dynasty.

　　Amber is a fossil formed through chemical changes in resin buried under the earth for millions of years.

琥珀童子斗蟋蟀图鼻烟壶

清中期
通高 7 厘米　宽 5.1厘米

　　绿料盖，银鎏金托，扁圆形壶身，呈棕红色，琥珀质。壶身两面分别浅浮雕有数名小童在庭院围栏间聚精会神的斗蟋蟀玩耍。雕刻的线条流畅，人物神态生动活泼，童趣盎然，是上乘之作。

Amber snuff bottle with pattern of children teasing crickets

Mid-Qing Dynasty
Overall height 7cm　Width 5.1cm

　　This bottle in reddish brown amber and green glass lid has reliefs depicting children teasing crickets inside a fence within a courtyard. The cutting flows freely, with the human figures lively and lifelike. The bottle is a masterpiece.

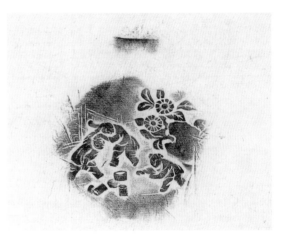
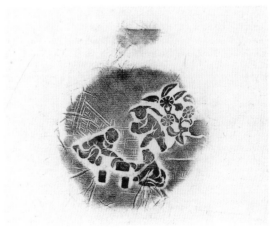

粉彩描金百子庆春图鼻烟壶

清乾隆
通高 6.2厘米　宽 4.7厘米

　　碧玺盖，扁圆形壶身，瓷胎粉彩。烟壶扁腹，两面描金开光，绘有"百子庆春"图，方寸间巧纳百人，神态各异，或敲锣、或舞龙、或吹号、或戏狮，一派生机喜庆景象。壶身两侧绘绿地粉彩花卉纹，底足内有"乾隆年制"四字篆书款。整体布局紧凑，繁而有序，是典型的乾隆官窑作品。

Famille rose snuff bottle with painting of 100 children celebrating spring

Qianlong Reign (1736~1795), Qing Dynasty
Overall height 6.2cm　Width 4.7cm

　　The flat famille rose bottle has an apyrite lid. The body of the bottle has a golden frame on its obverse and back, and each frame has a picture of children celebrating the arrival of spring. There are altogether around 100 children in the images. Some of the children are beating a gong and drums, one is playing a trumpet, and still others are performing lion and dragon dances. The jubilant scene is realistically portrayed. On both sides of the bottle are designs of red flowers on a green background. At its foot is the inscription, "Made in the Reign of Qianlong." The composition is tight and ordered. The bottle is a typical product of a government-run kiln during the Qianlong reign.

天青釉金彩十二生肖图鼻烟壶（一对）

清
通高 8.2厘米　宽 4.6厘米

　　蟠螭纹铜鎏金盖，扁瓶形壶身，瓷胎。壶身以天青釉作为底色，两面堆塑金彩十二生肖图案，动物形象生动活泼，相映成趣。烟壶颈部以圆形回纹作为装饰，两侧肩部则配以兽首铺耳。底足内有"乾隆年制"四字篆书款。整体布局有序，繁而不乱。

Azure glaze snuff bottle with gilded design of 12 animals (A pair)

Qing Dynasty (1644~1911)
Overall height 8.2cm　Width 4.6cm

　　The pair of porcelain snuff bottles, each with a lid with patterns of a *Chi*-dragon, is coated with azure glaze. On the ground are sculptures of 12 animals which have been used as signs for a cycle of 12 years. The animals are lifelike and lovely. The necks of the bottles are decorated with frets. On their shoulders are handles in the shape of animal faces. On the bottom is an inscription in seal script, "Made in the reign of Qianlong". The elaborate designs are united in an orderly composition.

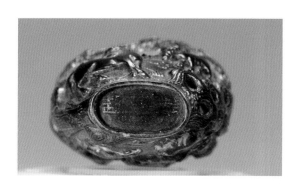

杂项篇Other Antique

翡翠荷叶式水丞

清中期
高 4.4厘米　长 9.5厘米

　　翡翠质，古朴凝练。此器为老坑翡翠整块随
形雕琢而成。盛夏的荷叶翻转，上趴俯着一只小松
鼠，利用翡的黄色巧雕而成，形态生动可爱，荷叶
下自由伸展的花蕾生机盎然，整体雕工熟练，制作
精美。下配紫檀木雕松竹梅随形底座，大气凝重，
为文人书房陈列把玩的精美之器。

Jadeite lotus-leaf shaped water container

Mid-Qing Dynasty
Height 4.4cm　Length 9.5cm

　　The vessel is made from a whole block of jadetie dug
from an old pit. In the shape of a lotus leaf with its edges
turned up, it has a sculpted squirrel on it, whose yellow
coloring is a spot on the jadeite. The animal is lifelike
and lovely, while the lotus leaf has buds extending freely
under it. The whole piece displays superb craftsmanship.
Beneath it is a purple sandalwood stand, carved into
bamboo, pine and plum, enhancing the vessel's beauty
and grandeur.

78

翡翠双狮钮衔环盖炉

清
高 13.5厘米　宽 14.5厘米

　　翡翠质，光洁圆润。炉盖上为太狮少狮戏珠钮，两狮相对而卧，嬉戏玩耍，形态可掬。两侧铺首为兽首衔环耳，刀法洗练。三足亦为狮子戏球状，活泼生动。此盖炉选料老坑翡翠，色泽浓厚，通体上下呼应，浑然天成。下配红木嵌银丝镂雕花卉底座，古朴大气，流畅简洁，为书房陈设品的上乘之作。

Jadeite lidded incense burner with two sculpted lions handles holding rings in trunks

Qing Dynasty (1644~1911)
Height 13.5cm　Width 14.5cm

　　The burner is made of smooth and bright jadeite. Its lid has a handle in the shape of two lions, one old and the other young, playing with a ball. The two lions sit face to face, and their facial expressions are lovely. At each of the two sides of the burner is an elephant's face holding a ring in its trunk. The burner is concisely carved. Each of its three feet is also in the form of an animal playing with a ball. The material used is jadeite dug from an old pit, so it is bright green. The whole burner is coherently conceived and executed. Under the burner is a mahogany stand which is embedded with silver filament, which has pierced designs of flowers. The burner with the impressive stand is a fine ornament for a study.

79

翡翠蝠衔灵芝钮印章

清
高 1.9厘米　长 3.2厘米

　　翡翠质，青翠温润。印章为老坑翡翠所雕琢，色艳，水分足。利用翡翠材质上的青白相间巧雕一蝙蝠口衔灵芝，雕刻技法娴熟、流畅。蝠衔灵芝为中国古代器物多采用的吉祥纹饰，寓意福寿安康之意。

Jadeite seal with a knob in the shape of a bat with glossy ganoderma in its mouth

Qing Dynasty (1644~1911)
Height 1.9cm　Length 3.2cm

　　The seal is carved from green and jadeite from an old pit, hence the brilliant color. The green and white parts on the jadeite were used to carve a bat with a glossy ganoderma in its mouth. The cutting was executed with skill and ease. A bat holding glossy ganoderma was traditionally used as an auspicious symbol, with a message of happiness and good health.

翡翠金鱼胸针

清
长 3.8厘米　宽 2.3厘米

　　翡翠质，色泽翠艳，水头足。仿若一弯碧水，雕刻出一条活泼可爱的金鱼在水中自在摆尾状，双面雕工，刀法洗练，整件器物立体而生动。底部镶金上有金行字号"北京恒丰九金谷"。原为挂坠，后改制成胸针。

Jadeite goldfish brooch

Qing Dynasty (1644~1911)
Length 3.8cm　Width 2.3cm

　　Carved out of brilliant jadeite, this lovely goldfish appears to be flicking its tail in the water. The goldfish is carved on both sides. The whole piece shows a vivid three-dimensional image. On the bottom is an inscription of the name of a gold shop, "Beijing Heng Feng Jiu Jin Gu." Originally a pendant, it was later reshaped into a brooch.

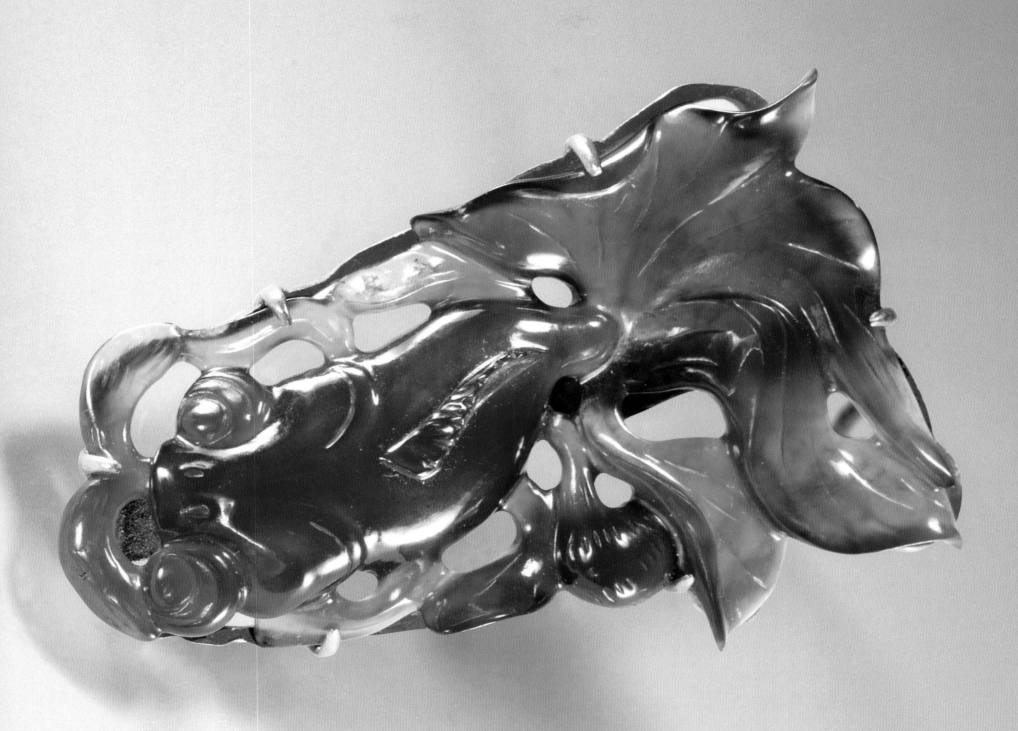

81

芙蓉石卧狮

清
高 4.6厘米　长 9.7厘米

　　芙蓉石质，圆润细致，采用整块芙蓉石料圆雕技法雕琢而成。少狮作俯卧状，双目圆睁，双足紧缩状，鬃尾和眉毛雕刻线条细腻流畅，造型生动，神态可人，多为文人摆玩之物，是清代芙蓉石摆件中的上佳之器。另配黄杨木镂雕竹石底座，上下浑然成为一体。

Rose quartz lying lion

Qing Dynasty (1644~1911)
Height 4.6cm　Length 9.7cm

　　The lion cub is sculpted from a block of smooth and fine rose quartz. The cub lies prone, with piercing eyes, and its paws drawn under it. Its mane and brows are finely carved. This lifelike and lovely creature was used as an ornament in scholars' studies. It is a fine piece produced during the middle of the Qing Dynasty. The boxwood stand with fretted patterns of bamboo and rocks appears to be an integral part of the sculpture.

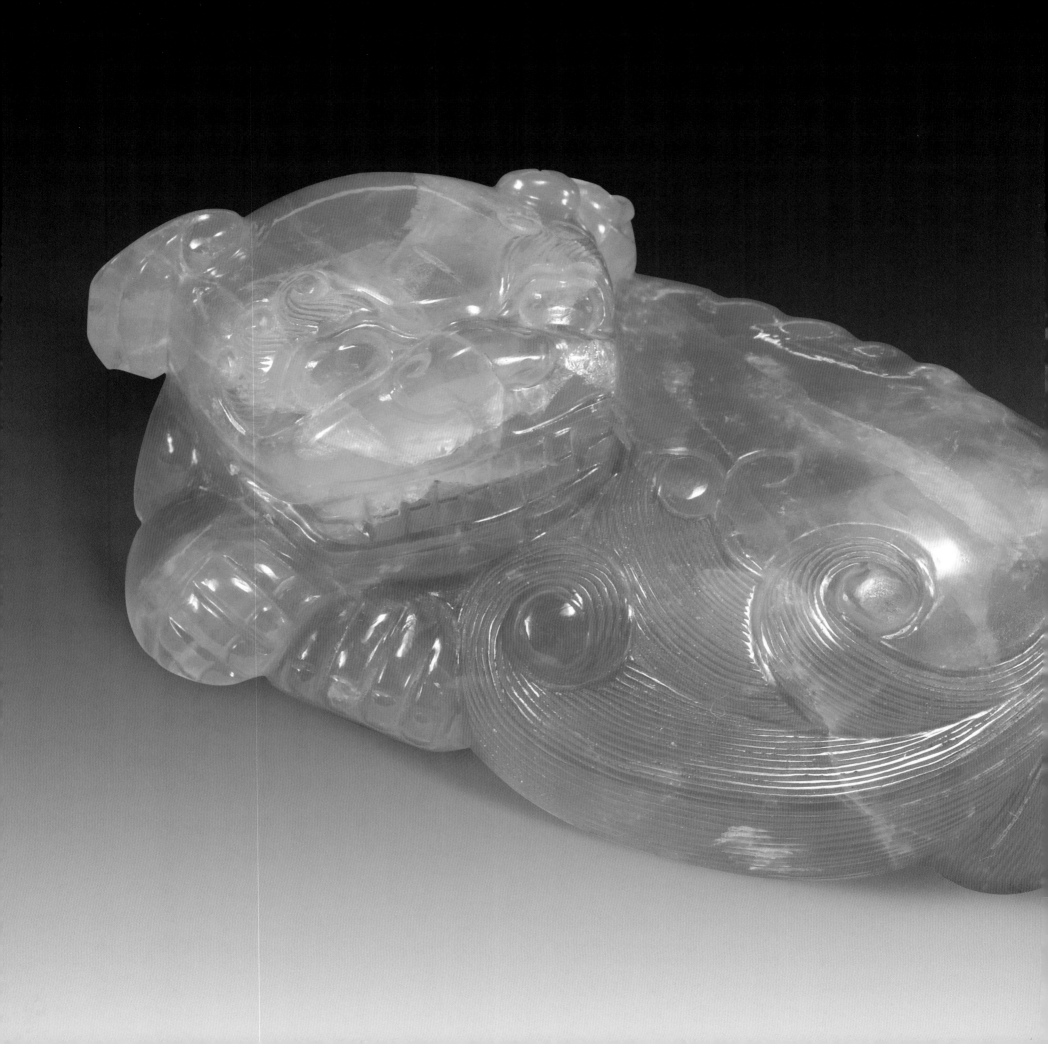

82

金嵌珍珠宝石挂坠

清晚期
长 6.6厘米　宽 4.1厘米

　　黄金质挂坠。其上镶嵌红碧玺、翡翠、蓝宝石，珍珠等宝石，整体造型似一片叶子，藤蔓缠绕，栩栩如生，整体造型动感活泼。

Gold pendant embedded with apyrite, jadeite, sapphire and pearl

Late Qing Dynasty
Length 6.6cm　Width 4.1cm

　　This gold pendant in the shape of a hanging leaf is embedded with apyrites, emeralds, sapphires, pearls and gems. The vines around it are realistically carved, adding vitality to the whole piece.

金嵌珍珠宝石手链

清晚期
长 15.7厘米　宽 1.9厘米

　　黄金质手链。其上嵌珍珠和翡翠相间成菱格纹样，边饰为珍珠、碧玺、翡翠相间的勾云纹。色彩上红绿相间，宛如红花绿叶相衬，此手链略有复古的味道。

Gold bracelet with embedded gem

Late Qing Dynasty
Length 15.7cm　Width 1.9cm

　　The gold bracelet has a rhombic design consisting of tiny pearls and a jadeite. At either side of the rhombic design is an arc formed by small pearls, jadeites and apyrites. The red and green colours bring out each other's beauty. The bracelet is done in an antique style.

84

金云龙纹手串

清
串口直径 9.8厘米　金珠直径 1.3厘米

　　纯金质串珠，中间隔片为虬角。手串的子珠均
为纯金錾刻云龙纹金珠，每颗珠上盘踞一条金龙，
双眼圆睁，鬃毛飞立，气势威武，为清代云龙纹样
式的典型特点。顶珠和母珠为桃红色碧玺，坠饰以
小米珠缠绕椭圆形碧玺装饰，记子留是以小米珠与
水滴状碧玺来装饰。中间的隔片为虬角，虬角片两
边打凹，中间起线，这也在细节上显示出整个手串
的精细和讲究，着实是件让人爱不释手之喜物。

Gold prayer beads with carved design of cloud and dragon

Qing Dynasty (1644~1911)
Round diameter 9.8cm　　Golden bead diameter 1.3cm

　　These prayer beads are all made of pure gold. Each
set of two beads is intersected with sea animal horn.
Each bead has a relief of a majestic winding dragon with
glaring eyes and flying mane, a typical Qing-dynasty
presentation of clouds and dragons. One pink apyrite bead
is inserted midway, and a large pink apyrite bead is tied to
the top of a tassel hanging from the rosary. The pendant
of the rosary is an oval piece of apyrite wound with tiny
pearls, as are the beads at the ends of the tassel strings.
The animal horn between every two beads is carved
concave at the centre on both sides so as to fit the beads.
This shows that particular attention was paid to all details
of the rosary when it was made.

85

银鎏金双龙戏珠纹扳指

清乾隆
高 2.9厘米　径 3.8厘米

　　银鎏金质，古拙凝重，金属感强烈。扳指上下雕刻回纹边饰，中间为鎏金錾花透雕双龙戏一（蜘）蛛——珠谐音，很有趣味性。整体布局井然有序，雕刻精细，地子琢磨平整，为清乾隆时期的典型之物。

Gilded silver thumb ring with two dragons playing with a spider

Qianlong Reign (1736~1795), Qing Dynasty
Height 2.9cm　Diameter 3.8cm

　　The gilded silver thumb ring exhibits the strong character of the metal. On the top and bottom of its exterior are bands of frets. The middle section is carved with two dragons playing with a spider. Dragons playing with a pearl was a common theme. Here the artist plays on the Chinese pronunciation for spider, (zhi) zhu, and the pearl, zhu. The carving's humor also derives from this pun. The decoration is finely carved with neat composition. The backdrop to the carving is polished smooth. All these are hallmarks of the carvings of the Qianlong era.

象牙西园雅集图笔筒

清早期
高 14.3厘米　口径 7.9厘米

象牙质，雕工精细。采用浅刻技法，主体纹饰为松树、远山、人物，房屋、小桥流水、假山，错落有致，仿若一幅人物山水画。描绘的是北宋汴京以苏轼为首的16位文人高士"西园雅集"时的情景，其中人物三三两两，或作诗绘画，或谈禅论道，栩栩如生。此器品质尚好，为清代文房清供的上品。

Ivory brush pot with engraving of a scholars' gathering at the Western Garden

Early Qing Dynasty
Height 14.3cm　Mouth diameter 7.9cm

The brush pot has an engraving of a gathering of the 11th-century scholar Su Shi and 15 other men of letters in the Western Garden. The main motifs are trees, mountains, human figures, houses, bridges, flowing water, and a rockery. The scholars in twos and threes are composing poems, painting, or talking about Buddhism and Daoism, all vividly represented. The well-preserved brush pot is a fine piece of Qing-dynasty stationery.

象牙月下书千卷图笔筒

清
高 10.4厘米　口径 5.7厘米

　　象牙质，温润细腻。整器截用整根象牙琢成，牙质洁白，温润如玉，运用线刻的技法，浅刻出远山、松石、阁楼，一文人雅士在阁内抚琴，山高水远，意境深远。并行书"月下书千卷"、"山人"、"竹"、"石"款。人物和景观相得益彰，生动跃然于笔下，仿若一张文人画。该器是清代象牙类书房陈设的佳品。

Ivory brush pot with the inscription of writing on 1000 rolls of paper in moonlight

Qing Dynasty (1644~1911)
Height 10.4cm　Mouth diameter 5.7cm

　　Carved from a smooth and fine white tusk, this brush pot bears incised images of mountains, pine, rocks, houses, and a scholar playing a plucked qin instrument inside a pavilion. An inscription on the pot reads, "Writing on 1,000 rolls of paper in moonlight," beside the colophons "Shanren (hermit)," "Zhu (bamboo)," and "Shi (rock)." With landscapes and human figures setting each off other, the whole picture embraces the style of Chinese literati painting. The brush pot is a fine piece of Qing-dynasty ivory stationery.

象牙龙凤纹针线筒

清
高 15.8厘米　口径 2.9厘米

　　象牙质，工艺上看是典型的广作。针线筒盖上浮雕游龙走凤图案，筒身采用浮雕工艺雕刻龙、云、百鸟图案，其中龙飞凤舞，百鸟朝凤，一派祥和安宁的景象；筒内放置各种型号的缝针。

　　在外销象牙工艺制品中，有许多欧式的针线盒，造型精美，应为当时欧洲皇室贵族的女眷们做刺绣针织的工具盒，里面有针线筒、线梭、刀、剪刀等各种精巧的工具。此器应为其中的一件针线筒，器物流畅，洗练，精美，小巧。

Ivory needle case with carved dragon and phoenix design

Qing Dynasty (1644~1911)
Height 15.8cm　Mouth diameter 2.9cm

　　The case features reliefs of dragons, clouds, and birds paying tribute to phoenixes, representing a scene of harmony and peace. On the lid are reliefs of a dragon and a phoenix. The whole case is small, beautiful and exquisitely manufactured.

　　Made in Guangdong for export, this exquisite European-style article was used by women in European imperial families. A container of needlework tools used by such women had in it smaller cases for needles, shuttles, knives, scissors, and other small implements. This object is a case for needles of different sizes.

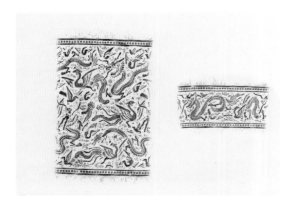

89

象牙雕竹节式喜鹊登梅图臂搁（一对）

清
长 6.5厘米　宽 2厘米

　　象牙质，精美细腻。为整块上等象牙雕琢而成，采用立体浮雕技法成竹节状，桠枝洁白如玉，臂搁外壁上浮雕竹叶、蜜蜂，内壁分别高浮雕喜鹊登梅图和鱼戏莲叶图。整体工艺精湛，选材考究，品质完好。

　　臂搁是古代文人用来搁放手臂的文案用具。除了能防止墨迹站在衣袖上外，垫着臂搁书写的时候，也会使腕部感到非常舒服，因此臂搁也称腕枕。是文人书房中实用把玩之佳品。此器较为小巧，应为臂搁式的文玩把件。

Ivory armrest with design of magpies alighting on a plum tree (A pair)

Qing Dynasty (1644~1911)
Length 6.5cm　Width 2cm

　　Carved from an entire superior tusk, these armrests were carved to resemble sections of a split bamboo stem, with reliefs of bamboo leaves and bees on the exterior of both halves, and deep reliefs of magpies alighting on a plum tree in the interior of one piece, and fish among lotus leaves in the other. These two armrests were produced with consummate skill from original ivory.

　　The armrest is a type of stationery for scholars to rest their arms while writing. Apart from preventing any ink blotting his sleeve, a writer feels comfortable when his arm is cushioned with an armrest. It is also an ornament for a scholar's study. Small armrests like these were admired for their beauty more than they were used as implements.

90

象牙仕女执花坐像

清
通高 18厘米　底径 9厘米 × 7.6厘米

　　象牙质，温润滑爽，雕工精细。整体采用立体
高浮雕技法，一清代仕女屈身坐在花园的假山石
上，只见她柳叶眉、丹凤眼、樱桃小嘴一点点，发
髻轻挽，身着薄衫，面容娇美，仪态安详，坐在山
石之上，左手执花，右手扶石，眉目传情，目光含
羞，体态婀娜，造型栩栩如生。整件器物雕刻技法
娴熟，人物仪态和神情捕捉的极为准确，其中衣
服、头发、花朵、花篮、山石均经染色处理，工艺
高超。下配象牙染色栅栏状红木底座，为清代象牙
制品摆件中的精美之器。

Ivory statuette of a lady holding a flower

Qing Dynasty (1644~1911)
Overall height 18cm　Bottom diameter 9cm×7.6cm

　　This deep relief in smooth and fine ivory represents
a Qing-dynasty lady sitting on a rock in a garden. Her
eyebrows are long and slender, her eyes slanting and her
lips ruby. With her hair up in a bun at the back of her
head, she wears a gauze jacket. The lady is pretty and
demure. She holds a flower in her left hand, and supports
herself with her right hand on the rock. She looks shy. Her
slender frame and her facial expression are realistically
and precisely depicted. Her clothing, hair, flower,
flower basket and rocks are collared. The whole piece is
skilfully carved. Beneath the statuette is a redwood stand
in the shape of a railing, tinted in an ivory hue. It is a
masterpiece of ivory sculpture produced during the Qing
Dynasty.

91

蜜蜡云鹤纹蛚子

清早期
高 5.6厘米　径 1厘米

　　蜜蜡质，质朴细腻。通体雕琢云鹤纹饰，两只展翅的仙鹤，遥遥相望，振羽欲飞状，古朴简练中有沉稳之气。

　　蜜蜡，为有机类矿物之一，质地脂润，色彩缤纷，以红色为上佳。在物理成分上和化学成分上都和琥珀没有区别，主要成分为松树脂，因"色如蜜，光如蜡"而得名。

Amber *Lezi* tube with design of cloud and crane

Early Qing Dynasty
Height 5.6cm　Diameter 1cm

　　The exterior of this amber tube is covered with a relief of clouds and two cranes gazing at each other, and flapping their wings. The concise relief is rendered in an ancient style.

　　Amber is an organic mineral, and red amber is regarded as superior. Its main content is resin.

92

犀角大鹏金翅鸟首印章

清中期
高 3.3厘米 底径 2.6厘米

犀角质，包浆润泽。采用立体雕刻技法而成，犀角纹理清晰，角质宁润，一大鹏金翅鸟趴俯状，首眺前方，欲腾飞跃起。

大鹏金翅鸟又作妙翅鸟，为印度教毗湿奴神所跨乘，是三世诸佛智慧与方便的显现。持有此枚金翅鸟印章寓意事业蒸蒸日上，祈愿此后也能利益等同虚空的诸方众生，是个祥瑞之物。

Rhinoceros horn seal with knob in the shape of a golden-winged roc

Mid-Qing Dynasty
Height 3.3cm Bottom diameter 2.6cm

Carved from rhinoceros horn with a smooth lustre and clear veins, the sculpture presents a roc looking forward and flapping its wings to fly upward.

The gold-winged roc is believed to be the Hindu god Vishnu's mount, and is a representation of the wisdom and insight of all Buddhas. Having a seal with the knob in the shape of this bird expresses the wish for the owner of the seal to have a successful career, and benefiting all living beings.

琥珀扳指

清中期
高 2.8厘米 宽 3.4厘米

　　琥珀质，温软细润，为整料琢成，表面依稀可见当初树脂流动时产生的纹路。扳指一面扁平，似为一烟碟，可谓一物两用，琢磨精细，光素无纹，地子平整，品质上佳，应为过去皇亲贵族喜好常备之物。

Amber thumb ring

Mid-Qing Dynasty
Height 2.8cm　width 3.4cm

　　This thumb ring is carved from a whole block of amber. On the surface are faintly visible signs of flowing resin. One side of the ring is flat, and that side may have been used as an ash holder. Finely polished, this thumb ring of fine-quality amber might have been a favourite object for the imperial family or aristocrats in the past.

94

紫檀松竹梅图笔筒

清
高 11.5厘米 口径 7.3厘米

　　紫檀质。整器用紫檀圆木整挖，精心雕琢而成。纹理细致紧密，光泽古朴深邃，仿树瘿状，上高浮雕松竹梅纹饰。

　　中国古代文人喜爱寄物抒情，借以来表现刚毅高尚的品格，坚毅不拔的青松，挺拔多姿的翠竹，傲雪报春的冬梅，三物都有不畏严寒的高洁风格，而誉为"岁寒三友"，以此比喻忠贞的友谊。整器凝重洗炼，大方古拙，为文人书房陈设常用之上等佳器。

Red sandalwood brush pot with design of pine, bamboo and plum tree

Qing Dynasty (1644~1911)
Height 11.5cm Mouth diameter 7.3cm

　　This brush pot was made by hollowing out a section of fine-grained redsandalwood and carving. With an antique lustre, it is in the shape of knotty wood with reliefs of a pine, a bamboo and a plum tree.

　　In ancient times, Chinese men of letters liked to convey their sentiments through objects. Pine is regarded as firm and resolute, and bamboo is compared to upright people, while plum trees are appreciated for braving the cold in winter. These three plants, known as "the three friends during cold seasons," are symbols of constant friendship. The brush pot with its simple form is a fine piece of stationery.

95

沉香木手串

清中期
串口直径 9.5厘米　珠子直径 1.35厘米

　　沉香木质。该手串由十八颗圆雕万字盘扣结沉香木籽串组成。顶珠和母珠均为红珊瑚质地，雕万字盘扣钮，坠饰为翡翠双面雕两条鲶鱼纹饰，上下用小米珠点缀。记子留两颗，一为黄碧玺，一为粉红碧玺。

　　沉香具有浓郁的香味，有降气温中，暖肾纳气之功效。《医林纂要》中记载："坚肾，补命门，温中、燥脾湿，泻心、降逆气，凡一切不调之气皆能调之。并治噤口毒痢及邪恶冷风寒痹。"手串的整体感觉大气凝重，令人爱不释手。

Eaglewood prayer beads

Mid-Qing Dynasty
Round diameter 9.5cm　Bead diameter 1.35cm

　　This rosary is made of 18 round eaglewood beads carved with designs of Buddhist swastika. The larger beads in the middle, and at the joint with the tassel, are of red coral, also carved with swastika designs. The pendant hanging from the rosary is carved with designs of two fish on both sides, with tiny beads as ornaments on top and beneath it. One bead at the end of the tassel is of yellow apyrite, and the other, pink apyrite.

　　Eaglewood emits a very strong sweet scent, and also has curative efficacy against certain ailments. Medical records claim it was used to cure malaria, aphasia, and diseases caused by cold wind. The whole rosary exudes simplicity and reverence.

剔红花果纹盒

清乾隆
高 3.9厘米　底径 6.7厘米×6.3厘米

　　木胎质，通体髹朱漆。采用剔红的技法剔出纹饰。整器朱色深红沉蕴，盒盖呈方形，上下开启，盒身为倭角正方形，通体万字锦地上深刻花果纹饰，瓜身为变形米字锦地纹，藤叶茂盛，瓜果绵绵。布局富丽堂皇，构图疏密得当。漆面平整，剔红层次均匀，工艺精湛，纹饰细致，刀法犀利流畅。是清代剔红器陈设品中的精品。

Lacquer box carved with design of fruit and flower

Qianlong Reign (1736~1795), Qing Dynasty
Height 3.9cm　　Bottom diameter 6.7cm×6.3cm

　　This rounded-square carmine box with a wooden base is coated with multiple layers of lacquer carved into reliefs. Designs of flowers and fruit are carved on a background covered with frets, and the fruit have adapted designs of the Chinese character "*Mi*." Smoothly varnished, the meticulously carved coating of the box reveals free and flowing traces of carving on even layers. With splendid ornamentation and rhythmic composition, it is a fine piece of Qing-dynasty red lacquer ware.

黄玻璃荷花形鸟食罐（一对）

清乾隆
高 2.8厘米　口径 5.3厘米

　　黄料质，晶莹剔透。器物所用的黄料中略闪绿色，俗称"西湖水"。器形精巧，琢刻细腻，鸟食罐呈八瓣形荷花状，下浮托在荷叶之上，鸟食罐的手柄处为红白套料浮雕，一个为渔耕图，另一个为肩担图。精致的造型和做工使这对原为提笼架鸟的使用之物，更为精巧，后配上手柄后成为一对把玩的小物件，让人爱不释手。

Yellow glass lotus-flower shaped bowls for bird food (A pair)

Qianlong Reign (1736~1795), Qing Dynasty
Height 2.8cm　Mouth diameter 5.3cm

　　Made from transparent yellow glass with a faint green sheen, this pair of bird food bowls was ingeniously conceived and meticulously produced, in the shape of an eight-petal lotus flower on a lotus leaf. On the handles of the containers are reliefs in red and white glass. One relief shows a fisherman, and the other a porter carrying a load with a shoulder pole. The beautiful form and excellent craftsmanship make these objects of daily use very attractive.

金地蓝彩回寿纹小杯（一对）

清道光
高 4.4厘米　口径 6.3厘米

　　金地蓝彩，胎质细腻，造型小巧。深腹，内壁
素白，外施金彩，圈足。通体呈现富丽堂皇之气，
器身有蓝料彩绘四螭龙团寿纹，色彩浓烈，釉面肥
润，凝重中彰显皇家御器的庄严。底足内有"大清
道光年制"六字篆书款，为道光官窑的上品之作。

Porcelain cup with design of dragon and a circularized "*Shou*" character in blue glaze on gold ground (A pair)

Daoguang Reign (1821~1850), Qing Dynasty
Height 4.4cm　Mouth diameter 6.3cm

　　The fine porcelain cups have circular bases at
the bottom. Their interiors are white. The exterior is
painted gold colour. Each of the splendid cups has
four circularized Chinese *Shou* (longevity) characters
surrounded by *Chi*-dragons. The designs are painted with
blue enamel. The strong colour and rich enamel coating
set off the grandeur of the imperial ware. At the bottom
of the cups are inscriptions in seal script, reading, "Made
during the Daoguang Reign, Qing Dynasty". They are fine
pieces produced in official kiln.

图版索引

Index of Plates

《心悦雅集》小传

黑静麟

古玩收藏近二十载，成败喜忧，多有心得，难抑心中冲动，欲与知音分享。适逢近有闲暇，遂将近百珍宝，汇集整理，承蒙朋友相助，师长帮扶，划为美玉、烟壶、杂项三篇，精雕细琢，成就《心悦雅集》，实现几代人夙愿。

我与夫人，虽非望族之后，但家庭浸淫古董珍玩，已是四代传承，"德义兴"、"乐天商行"早在清末民初，就已名满京城。置身如斯家庭，父辈言传身教，指点迷津，自身耳濡目染，勤学苦练，眼力、灵性突飞猛进。

美玉无瑕，五德高雅，其仁爱、忠义、智慧、勇气、廉洁，亦为人生所需，收藏美玉，成为我们古董珍玩的首选。

《心悦雅集》中收录的白玉麒麟绶带鸟摆件，是我心爱之物。收藏此物，既有机缘巧合，又是性情所致。此摆件造型出神入化，应属明代宫廷之物，细观玉质，晶莹剔透、温和滋润，雕工精美细腻，面目表情栩栩如生。绶带鸟温顺飘逸，体态典雅，富贵之气，浑然天成；麒麟口衔天书，回首仰望，双目炯炯，气宇轩昂，尽显天兽之霸气，令人肃然起敬。加之麒麟与静麟取名之缘，故而收藏之心蠢蠢欲动，欲罢不能，几番夜不能寐，最终收入囊中。每日沾沾自喜，爱不释手，竟有日久生情之感。

人养美玉，美玉养人。藏玉，让我们忘记许多烦恼，其超凡脱俗、圆润包容的品格，时时刻刻净化着我们浮躁的心灵。

星移斗转，白驹过隙。随着时间的推移，我们的眼界在开阔，视野更长远。随着收藏领域的拓宽，翡翠、鼻烟壶、象牙、犀角等杂项也开始成为我们青睐之物。

书中那只巧夺天工的玻璃胎画珐琅开光西洋山水人物图鼻烟壶，成为我高山仰止的镇宅之宝。这只乾隆时期由清宫造办处烧制的鼻烟壶做工十分考究。簪花铜鎏金盖，扁圆形壶身，涅白色玻璃胎上施珐琅彩，

椭圆形圈足。壶体两面开光，开光内以胭脂色绘西洋山水人物楼阁图案，开光外以黄色绘卷草纹，底足内阴刻"乾隆年制"四字楷书款。此壶图纹应为宫廷画家或西洋画家摹仿西洋画法所绘，形式新颖，做工精致。从造型到画片，独树一帜。烧制工艺纷繁复杂，胭脂水与料胎烧制温差二三十度，或高或低，必致前功尽弃，画片落笔之时，凸于表面，及至烧制完成，便如同印于料胎之上，抚之如砥。如此妙到毫巅之手笔，非寻常工匠可为之。

除器物本身稀有且价值不菲外，其中更饱含深情厚谊，友人情怀。此壶当初为好友、国家文物鉴定委员会委员、原北京文物公司瀚海艺术品拍卖公司总经理秦公先生，慧眼识真，高瞻远瞩，以胆识魄力力争，才使其免于漂泊海外，因而对这只鼻烟壶的喜爱，既有对其本身的倾心向往，更有对秦公先生的肺腑追思，相比那只玉麒麟绶带鸟摆件，更让我心痒难耐，寝食难安。当在拍卖会上最终落追，这件宝贝成为我囊中之物时，激动之情，难以言表。

一份珍藏，一段机缘。打开《心悦雅集》，展于您眼前的每一件珍藏，都是我心中挚爱。当初相遇之时，或内涵丰富，或惟妙惟肖，皆令我驻足流连，欣喜若狂。每一件珍藏，都像是我心爱的孩子，我们之间的情感，剪不断、理还乱。

收藏，修身养性；收藏，淡泊明志。亦收亦藏之中，情趣盎然，净化心灵，更生出些许感悟——收藏不在乎价值多少，不强调数量的堆积，努力追求独到精美，努力发现细微处蕴含的高超技艺。

现在，我的孩子们都对祖国的传统文化产生了浓厚的兴趣，在《心悦雅集》的酝酿过程中，也融入了他们的智慧和汗水。

国之精粹，我辈必将传承。

我们谨以《心悦雅集》与天下知音共赏。

The Story of Objects of Art from and for the Heart

Hei Jinglin

I have been dedicated in the collecting of antiques for almost 20 years. While I have enjoyed success, more than a few of my endeavours have ended in failure. Yet I have learned a great deal from this passion of mine, and on reviewing my experiences I feel I should share my experience with friends. Having had more free time lately, I have gathered photographs of nearly 100 objects from my collection into a book. With help of mentors and friends, I have classified these objects into categories such as jade articles, snuff bottles and other antiques, and titled the book, *Objects of Art from and for the Heart*. To *publish* such a book has long been a cherished wish of my family for generations.

My wife and I are not from prominent families, but our love of antiques has been passed down continuously through four generations. Early in the 20th century, the antiques shops "De Yi Xing" ("virtue, righteousness and thriving business") and "Le Tian Shang Hang" ("optimism shop") enjoyed wide repute in Beijing. Having grown up in such families, we have received guidance from our forebears. Through diligent education and solid practice, our ability to discern antiques has improved in leaps and bounds.

Jade, in Chinese people's mind, symbolizes five virtues: kindness, righteousness, wisdom, courage, and honour. These virtues are what humans need also, such that jade works have been our first choice for collection.

The auspicious creatures, the *qilin* and the *paradise* flycatcher bird, sculpted in white jade, as shown in this book,

is my favourite. It was acquired by chance, but it was also what I had long sought after. This vividly carved sculpture was once displayed in the Ming-dynasty (1368~1644) imperial palace. As I observed it I came to realize it was cut from smooth and translucent jade. This artefact exhibits breath-taking craftsmanship. The features of the creatures are lifelike. The gentle and graceful paradise flycatcher has a natural air of nobility. The *qilin*, with a book in its mouth, turns its head to look upward, its two eyes gleaming. It inspires awe among those who see it. Moreover, the "lin" in my name "Hei Jinglin" comes from the creature's name, *qilin*. The moment I glimpsed this jade artwork, I could not get it out of my mind, even dreaming of it at night. In the end, I paid a huge price for it. I grew very excited at this new find for my collection. I became so fond of it that I could not put it down. By and by I have developed a deep love for it.

Humans preserve fine jade; and in turn, fine jade inspires humans. In the collecting of jade, we forget worldly concerns. The unearthly, smooth and gentle quality of jade purifies the human heart, which would otherwise be impetuous.

With the passage of time, our vision has broadened and we have extended our collection to include emeralds, snuff bottles and other antique objects. An ingeniously manufactured opaque white glass snuff bottle with landscape and human figures painted in light rose enamel, as depicted in *Objects of Art from and for the Heart*, is the prize item in our collection. Produced with marvellous craft in the Palace Workshop during the reign of Emperor Qianlong (1736~1795), the flat bottle has a circular base. The bottle has bordered pictures of a European landscape with human figures on its front and back. Outside the borders is winding vines in yellow. At the bottom is the inscription, "Made during the Reign of Qianlong," carved in intaglio. The lid of the bottle is gilded and decorated with sculpted designs of flowers. The bottle was presumably painted by Chinese court artists or other artisans in the style of Europe paintings, or it could have even been executed by foreign artists. Both the bottle itself and its decoration are unique.

At that time, snuff bottles were produced in Palace Workshop either according to designs approved by the emperor or using designs created by artisans. The bottle in question was made by the latter. Firing such snuff bottles in imperial kilns was an extremely complicated and difficult process. There was a difference of 20 to 30 degrees centigrade in temperature for firing the bottle and the enamel coating. Too high or too a low temperature could spoil the entire bottle. When applied to the glass body, the designs were raised on the surface. When the bottle was fired, the designs lay flat on the smooth surface as if imprinted on the glass body. Such a technique was beyond the average artisan's ability. There has been only one bottle of this type found in the world so far, which has hence enhanced its value. Apart from its value, the bottle is a token of friendship. It was my good friend Qin Gong, former member of the National Cultural Relics Appraisal Committee, general manager of the Beijing Hanhai Auction Co. Ltd., who, with his keen eye and great determination, tried his best to keep the bottle from going abroad. So my love for this bottle comes from its beauty and also from my memory of Qin Gong. In comparison to the jade qilin, this snuff bottle enduringly lingered in my mind. I could hardly go to sleep or even eat for some time. I was apprehensive until I acquired it at an auction. My excitement went beyond words when the bottle became an item in my own collection.

Every object you see in *Objects of Art from and for the Heart* is imbued with my deep love. When I first saw these priceless objects, I was fascinated by their beautiful form and profound cultural substance. Each of them was added to my collection at a fortuitous opportunity. They are like my children. My love for them is profound and unfailing.

Collecting antiques helps cultivate character. Collectors should be indifferent to fame and wealth. With a purified mind, one comes to understand that it is not the size of one's collection, but the beauty contained within it that is significant.

My first son Chunyi and second son Chun'en have also developed an interest in traditional Chinese culture. They have participated in the preparation of this book.

We must inherit and preserve the finest of our national culture.

I am happy to share *Objects of Art from and for the Heart* with all who have similar interests to ours.

编后记

黑静麟

　　《心悦雅集》自酝酿之初，已历经数载。书中广收精选，所涵盖的内容、品类甚为广杂，几易其稿，梳理成章。对不同时期、各种品类、各种材质的玉器，烟壶和杂项做了较为系统的阐述。阅后给人丰而不杂、广而不泛之感。

　　《心悦雅集》曾得到过傅熹年先生、夏更起先生、王时麒先生及北京市文物进出境鉴定所专家们的大力支持和热情帮助。在此，我与夫人要向他们连同所有为本集出版付出辛劳的编辑、摄影以及蔡伟先生、黄振海先生、王利民先生等，一并致以诚挚的谢意。

Postscript

Hei Jinglin

　　Several yeas have passed since we began to prepare the album *Objects of Art from and for the Heart* and the manuscript has been rewritten time and again. The album contains introduction of jade articles, snuff bottles and other cultural relics made of different materials and dating to different periods of time in the past. The authors present them systematically so that the reader will be impressed by the rich contents but will not be puzzled by excessive details.

　　Fu Xinian, Xia Qigeng, Wang Shiqi and some specialists in Beijing Examination Institute of Imported and Exported Cultural Relics have given us generous help and support. Here we extend our heartfelt thanks to all editors and the photographer of the book as well as Cai Wei, Huang Zhenhai and Wang Limin who have made enormous contribution to the publication of this album.